Signalling Success

Paper-free approaches to recognising and recording learner progress and achievement

Alastair Clark and Shubhanna Hussain-Ahmed

niace

promoting adult learning

Published by the National Institute of Adult Continuing Education (England and Wales)
21 De Montfort Street
Leicester
LE1 7GE
England

Company Registration Number: 2603322
Charity Registration Number: 1002775

First published 2006
© NIACE 2006

NIACE has a broad remit to promote lifelong learning opportunities
for adults. NIACE works to develop increased participation in education
and training, particularly for those who do not have easy access
because of barriers of class, gender, age, race, language and culture,
learning difficulties and disabilities, or insufficient financial resources.

For a full catalogue of NIACE's publications, please visit www.niace.org.uk/publications

Cataloguing in Publications data
A CIP record for this title is available from the British Library.

ISBN (ten): 1 86201 251 2
ISBN (thirteen): 978 1 86201 251 6

Designed and typeset by Boldface, London
Printed by and bound in Great Britain by Latimer Trend

Contents

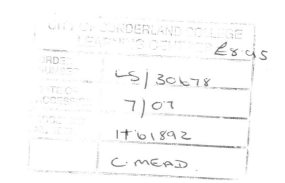

Acknowledgement iv
Foreword – Nick Bailey v
About this book vi

Chapter 1
Learner progress and achievement:
The RARPA process 1

Chapter 2
Applying digital technology to the
RARPA process 4

- RARPA Stage 1: setting learning aims
  appropriate to an individual learner or
  group of learners 4

- RARPA Stage 2: Initial assessment to
  establish the learner's starting point 5

- RARPA Stage 3: Identification of
  appropriately challenging learning
  objectives: initial negotiated and revised 7

- RARPA Stage 4: Recognition and recording
  of progress during programme (formative
  assessment): tutor feedback to learners,
  learner reflection and progress reviews 10

- RARPA Stage 5: End-of-programme
  learner self-assessment; tutor summative
  assessment; review of overall progress
  and acfhievement 13

Chapter 3
Planning to use technology 17

- The purpose of the technology 17
- Usability 17
- Accessibility 18
- Availability of the technology 18
- Learners' permissions 18
- Managing the data recorded 18
- Training 19
- Cost of implementing and using technology 29

Chapter 4
Digital devices for sight and sound 20

- Digital photographs 20
- Digital video 23
- Audio recordings 25
- Personal Digital Assistants (PDAs) 27

Chapter 5
Tools for asking questions 29

- Online quiz tools 29
- Online self-assessment tools 31
- Interactive voting software 32

Chapter 6
Digital learning spaces 35

- Blogs 35
- Learning platforms 37
- E-portfolios 38

Chapter 7
Making it happen 41

References 42

Books 42

Useful online resources 42

Glossary 44

Appendix 1 – Paper-free RARPA? A framework
for discussion 46

Appendix 2 – Example permission statement
from learner 47

Appendix 3 – List of participants in Technology
and Learning Outcomes pilot project 2004–05 49

Acknowledgements

We would like to thank the pilot projects that took part in the Learning Outcomes project and shared and disseminated the practice that they were developing around the use of various new technologies to record learner progress and achievement. We would also like to thank colleagues at NIACE and the Learning and Skills Council (LSC) for their input, and Brendan Donovan and Alan Clarke for their useful comments.

We would like to acknowledge the use of screen captures of Microsoft Applications in this book and to Dana McLaughlin, Sarah Perry, and Emily Bowman for providing photographs.

This publication has been supported by 'New Measures of Success' at the LSC – part of 'Success for All'.

Foreword

This publication draws lessons from the pioneering work which NIACE undertook with a group of organisations using new technologies to record progress and achievement. These pilots have helped to advance our understanding of how we can be more effective in recording learning.

The work has some very powerful messages for learning providers. We have seen how learners' progress and achievement can be recorded in unobtrusive ways that are appropriate and fit for purpose, make learning fun and really help learners understand their starting point, their progress and their achievement. This work has illustrated some excellent practice in the application of RARPA that is now being made more widely available and from which other organisations and practitioners can gain. It has also promoted the use of Information Learning Technology (ILT) in areas where traditionally little inroad has been made by technology and shows that with a little effort and imagination learning can be exciting, progress seen instantly and learners invigorated. I hope that this work encourages many more learning providers to experiment with what are becoming proven techniques for enhancing learning and the learner's experience.

Nick Bailey *Senior Policy Manager – Quality*
Widening Adult Participation
Learning and Skills Council

About this book

Recognising and recording the progress and achievement of learners is central to good teaching practice. Initial and ongoing assessment are both very important to this as they allow teachers to monitor their learners' progress as well as adapt their own teaching input. It is also important for learners themselves to be able to recognise their own progress, celebrate their successes and identify their challenges to learning.

Methods of recording an individual learner's progress and achievement need to be fit for purpose and meaningful to the learner. Using digital technology is one way to make this process more engaging and learner-centred.

This book has been written to share some of the practical lessons learned by tutors of adults who have used digital technology to record learner progress and achievement. It will raise issues for discussion, offer examples of how the technology can be used effectively and encourage the reader to find applications of technology that will work for their learners.

The content of this book is intended primarily for tutors and managers who are involved in delivering non-accredited learning to adults. However, the principles and practices of using technology to record progress apply equally to accredited provision and to all sectors of education.

1 Learner progress and achievement: the RARPA process

The recording of learners' progress and achievement is a fundamental element of good teaching practice. The importance of this has been recognised by the Learning and Skills Council (LSC) and from September 2006 providers who deliver non-accredited adult learning in England have had processes in place to record learner progress and achievement. (LSC, 2005)

Providers have been encouraged by the LSC to adopt the RARPA process (Recognising and Recording Progress and Achievement) in non-accredited learning. RARPA suggests the following five-staged approach:

1. Establishing aims appropriate to an individual learner or group of learners.
2. Understanding initial assessment to establish the learner's starting point.
3. Identifying appropriately challenging learning objectives: initial, renegotiated and revised.
4. Recognising and recording of progress and achievement during programme (formative assessment): tutor feedback to learners, learner reflection and progress reviews.
5. Carrying out end-of-programme learner self-assessment; tutor summative assessment; review of overall progress and achievement. This will be in relation to appropriately challenging learning objectives identified at the beginning and during the programme. It may include recognition of learning outcomes not specified during the programme.

Providers are expected to demonstrate that quality teaching and learning is taking place. The five-staged process contributes to this with its strong emphasis on meeting the individual needs of each learner. The process inevitably involves the collection of evidence of progress. It is important that this process is integrated within the teaching and learning activities and not seen as an external administrative requirement.

Providers who have used the five-staged process have reported that learners are enthusiastic about setting goals and following progress towards them. The benefits identified by learners included better motivation, faster progress and better engagement in learning (Greenwood and Wilson, 2004). Findings from the RARPA pilot also suggested that the process has benefits for learners who have previously had negative experiences of learning, with many of the learners reporting increased self-confidence and a more positive attitude to learning.

Why use digital technology to record learner progress and achievement?

Initially many providers were concerned that the recording of progress and achievement would lead to an increase in paper-based recording processes and bureaucracy. However, it is important to note that the RARPA staged process was never intended to be an exercise in form-filling as this can defeat the purpose of having a system which is learner-centred, non-bureaucratic and 'fit for purpose'.

Providers have experimented with the creation of paper documents to aid evidence collection at each of the five stages of RARPA. These have included Individual Learning Plans, learner diaries, quizzes and tests, and self-assessment activities.

Paper-based recording methods may not always be the most appropriate or useful approaches to recording a learner's progress and achievement. For example:

- Learners may not be comfortable filling out forms because of language or literacy issues.
- Forms may not be appropriate in classes where learners spend the majority of the time engaged in an activity (i.e. swimming, dancing and pottery).
- Paper forms can become associated with tedious administrative tasks unconnected with the learning process.

Imaginative use of technology can make the process of recording progress and achievement a more personalised experience for the learner and in some instances less time-consuming for the tutor, for example, much of the quiz software available can administer assessments (initial, formative and summative) and mark and analyse the learners' results.

Tutor competence in using the chosen technology is crucial for success. Its use must be 'seamless' and fit naturally into the flow of a learning session. Nervousness or reluctance in using the technology on the part of the tutor will easily transfer to reticence on the part of the learners to participate. For this reason tutors must be well trained in both the technical functions of the device or software and in the effective application of the technology to documenting progress and achievement.

Electronic evidence should be seen to be useful to the learners and not collected in ways that are unnecessarily intrusive. Learners should be given access to any of the evidence collected about their progress and ideally they should take ownership of any recording of their work and achievements.

There should be clear limits on the use to which the evidence can be put. Items such as learner comments and images of products may prove to be useful for other purposes such as staff training and marketing. Separate permission should be sought before materials are used for any other purpose beyond direct support of the learning process. Appendix 1 offers some possible wording of an agreement on the use of learners' work and recordings.

To confirm the ownership of the digital evidence at the end of a course, it may be appropriate to offer learners the opportunity to take away their own material using an appropriate medium. For example, documents and images with small file sizes could be e-mailed, larger assets may need to be placed on a CD or memory stick. In some instances, learners who do not have access to a computer at home may actually prefer to have paper print-outs of all their work.

In summary, digital evidence should be produced with the learner in mind and ultimately to help the learner to recognise and keep a record of their progress and their achievements.

2 Applying digital technology to the RARPA process

This chapter will explore some of the ways that technology can be applied to support each part of the RARPA staged process. Imaginative practitioners are finding new ways of harnessing digital technologies. The applications illustrated here should be seen as examples, but there are more uses waiting to be discovered!

All five stages of the RARPA process are considered separately. However, the particular benefit of digital technology is that it offers links between the stages and gives close integration with the learning process. Chapters 4, 5 and 6 give more detailed information on the types of hardware and software that can be used. The technical terms can be found in the Glossary.

RARPA Stage 1:
Setting learning aims appropriate to an individual learner or group of learners

The provider will usually set the general aim of a course prior to recruitment of learners. This initial programme offer has to be carefully expressed to be sure to be 'in tune' with the needs of potential learners. Close links with the community play an important part in formulating the general aims for a course. Useful information can be gleaned from potential learners through outreach activities. In developing a programme that is responsive to learners' needs the provider can use a range of methods to collect information and these can include web-based surveys, local online discussion forums and interactive voting systems.

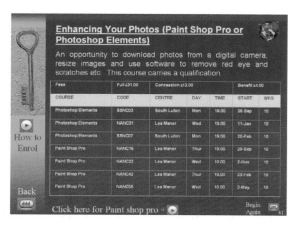

Screenshots from Luton Adult Education's guidance resource

Discussions over the aims of a course are often carried out as part of pre-course guidance involving reception staff or specialised guidance workers. Potential learners should have access to the detailed course aims in advance of the induction session. Having all course details with a clear set of course aims on the provider's website or intranet will assist remote access. It may also be possible to arrange for queries to be emailed to tutors prior to the course starting.

Luton Adult Education Service has developed a guidance resource to help their potential learners to find the most suitable ICT course for them. The resource asks a series of questions about the learners' previous experience of using computers and the internet and whether they have done any ICT courses before. Based on the responses, the resource lists possible courses that the learner can enrol on, with details of the course aims, and provides practical information on where and how to enrol. The resource can be used on a CD and learners can do it in their own time at home or at a learning centre. It can also used by office staff taking enrolments, allowing them to identify the most appropriate course, based on the responses that the potential learner provides.

RARPA Stage 2:
Initial assessment to establish the learner's starting point

Initial assessments are essential if a tutor is to understand how best to deliver a course to her/his learners. It is an area highlighted by the majority of the Learning Outcomes pilot projects and one in which technology can potentially play an important role.

Initial assessments can help to identify a learner's initial understanding of a subject and to find out what they would like to achieve. It is also an opportunity to find out if the learner has any additional support needs to help them to learn and progress in their course.

There can be two distinct approaches to initial assessment:

- self-assessment – where learners are asked to indicate their level of skill or knowledge
- objective testing – where learners are given tasks or questions to test their ability and knowledge.

Some initial assessment combines the two.

Current examples of paper-based initial assessments tend to be tick-based forms where learners self-assess or where tutors complete the forms on behalf of the learner following some initial discussions.

However, paper forms can be impractical to use, especially in courses such as swimming, yoga and dancing. Learners generally do not like taking time out of their lesson to fill out initial assessment forms, especially if the purpose of these forms is not obvious to them.

Initial assessments are a crucial part of the teaching and learning process. They need to be fit for the purpose of the learner and the course they are following. If learners understand the reason(s) for the initial assessment, then they are more likely to find it to be a more relevant and meaningful process.

Whilst assessing a learner's starting point it is also essential to include an assessment of the individual's needs to complete the course successfully. Where a method or technology is not accessible to a particular learner then it is essential that reasonable adjustment be made. Digital technology can offer a wide range of solutions.

Video recorders in sports and fitness

In Week One of a beginners' badminton course, learners are asked to play against each other without any instructions given on how to use a shuttlecock and racquet. The tutor uses a digital camcorder to record each of the learners. This allows her to assess their prior knowledge and skills. The video is played back to each learner individually.

The video clips provide an objective assessment of the learner's level of skill and abilities and can be used as the basis of discussion for initial assessment and for negotiating with the learner challenging learning objectives.

Seeing themselves in the video clip also gives learners a better understanding of what they are able to achieve and what areas of their game need improvement. Further on in the course, the tutor can film them again as part of their formative assessment and view the film with the learner. This allows them to discuss where there have been improvements and weaknesses that could be addressed. As part of the summative assessment, the tutor films the learners playing a badminton match against other learners. She also allows the learners to view all the previous weeks' footage so that learners can see how their techniques have improved during the course. For a learner to see for themselves the improvement in their game is quite powerful and can instil a sense of confidence and self-esteem.

Use of quizzes to assess starting point

Quizzes can be used to assess what a learner already knows about a subject and also what it is that they would like to know more about. Initial assessment quizzes can be administered using various methods such as:

● **An interactive voting system.** This will display the questions on a whiteboard and learners can respond using buttons on their handsets.
● **Personal Digital Assistants.** The tutor can have the questions on his or her PDA and beam these using a wireless link to the individual learners. The learners can then view the questions on their PDAs and beam back their responses.

- **Multiple-choice on a text document.** Tick boxes on a word-processed document can be completed on screen and saved or printed.
- **Quiz software.** Quiz software such as Hot Potatoes or Question Tools can be used to create quizzes.
- **Online survey.** Questions can be asked using software such as Quia or Survey Monkey.

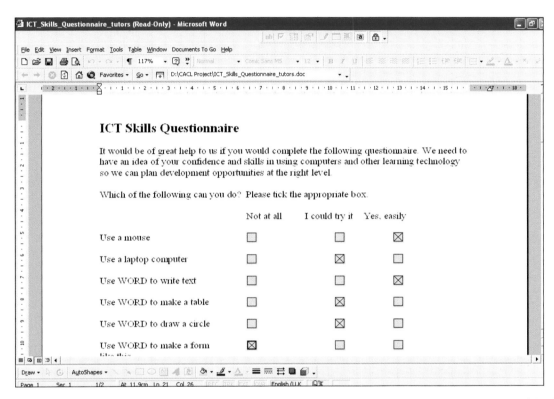

An example of a self-assessment using checkboxes created in Microsoft Word by Medway

RARPA Stage 3:
Identification of appropriately challenging learning objectives: initial, renegotiated and revised

Objectives are specific and detailed statements, which are used to identify the skills and knowledge that a learner would need to acquire in order to achieve their course aims.

A tutor can use the results of the initial assessment (Stage 2) as a basis for a discussion where objectives are agreed with each learner. These objectives can be recorded in text or oral form and then reviewed during the course and amended if this is appropriate.

Using audio recorders to document learning objectives

A conversation with the learner at the start of the course can be really useful for understanding their needs and motivations in wanting to learn. Tutors often find that it can be distracting to try and make notes while attempting to give their full attention to what the learner is saying. A small audio recording device can be used to record the conversation. The tutor can listen to it after the session and note particular students' needs and requirements. For learners who are not comfortable with filling out forms an audio recorder is a useful alternative to recording a learner's aims and goals for a course. At the end of the course (Stage 5 of RARPA), the learner can listen back to their initial aims and goals and reflect on whether they had achieved these objectives.

Its important that learners are comfortable with talking into an audio recorder and comfortable talking in front of the other learners. One way to do this is to have an 'icebreaker' where learners work in pairs or groups where they practise recording each other.

Explain to learners:

- the purpose of the recording
- how it will be used
- who will have access to it.

By retaining the recordings until the end of the course learners can listen back to their initial statement of aims and reflect on how far these have been achieved.

Recording and reflecting on learning objectives

At the initial session of a class, learners introduced themselves in a group and said what they hoped to gain from the course. A small voice recorder was passed round the room so that each set of individual aims were captured.

Free audio software was used to edit each contribution into a sound file for each learner. This took about half an hour but in doing this, the tutor was able to listen again to each of his learners.

A mid-term 'tutorial' was held after five weeks and each learner was offered the chance to listen again to his or her original goals. This stimulated a discussion of 'distance travelled' and promoted reflective thinking on the progress of the course and the re-setting of amended goals.

Recording and revisiting learning objectives using 'blogs'

Blogs (or weblogs, see page 35) offer a good way for learners to list their learning objectives at the start of the course. At the end of each class they can spend a few minutes reflecting on how they got on in the class that week and whether they have achieved their learning objectives for that day. If they have access to the Internet at home then they may make further entries on their blog.

Following a paper-based initial self-assessment exercise in a level 1 German language class, learners agreed their learning goals with the tutor and posted these in English to the first entry on their blog. Every week after that, the learners used the blog to post two separate entries:

1. **Meine Woche** – a paragraph in German describing what they had done that week
2. **My learning** – a paragraph in English summarising what they had learned that week and areas for additional work.

At the end of the term, the 'comments' section of the blog was set live and group members invited to comment on each other's progress. The tutor placed the final comment.

Using an e-portfolio to manage evidence of progress and achievement

An e-portfolio offers an opportunity to collect diverse evidence in one place. Where the portfolio is online this can be accessed from any web-connected PC. The learner can define who can view each element of the portfolio. Selected evidence can be used for potential employers or as part of an application to a higher-level course.

Flower arranging

At the start of a flower-arranging course each learner posted his or her agreed course objectives onto their learner portfolio. Each week the learners uploaded a photograph of their arrangement for that week. Against the picture learners commented on their progress and set themselves targets for the next week. At the end of the course the learners in discussion with the tutor chose their 'best' arrangements and set the permissions on the e-portfolios to allow other members of their class to view their final arrangements. A link was also placed to them from the 'Achievement' page of the provider's public website.

RARPA Stage 4:
Recognition and recording of progress and achievement during programme (formative assessment): tutor feedback to learners, learner reflection and progress reviews

Formative assessment is used to measure progress during a course. If used well it will not only motivate learners by identifying how much they have learned but it will also provide evidence of areas where objectives have not been met and where additional learning activities are needed. This stage covers the whole period of the course. The achievements will relate to the individual's goals (RARPA Stage 3) and can be measured against the initial assessment (RARPA Stage 2).

Digital images to improve performance

A digital image can provide a very swift way of recording the performance of a learner. Detailed images can provide instant feedback to learners on performance of a physical skill. Also some cameras offer the opportunity to take multiple pictures in swift succession, which can freeze action at several points within a movement.

Improving dance steps

In a dance class a learner who is having difficulty mastering a particular dance step can have a series of photographs taken by the tutor whilst going through the dance step. The images can then be shown to the learner and used as the basis of discussion for areas of improvement for the learner.

Capturing learners' movements to feed back on performance

Learners using blogs to write reflective learning diaries

Learners can keep diaries online in the form of a weblog or blog. Individuals can add to their personal learning objectives (Stage 3) and record the factual details of what happened. An even richer experience will come from adding reflections on the learning progress. Blogs can also allow tutors or peers to add comments and this can also enhance the process. Here is an example.

EXAMPLE 'BLOG'

Nature of BLOG entry
Example
Contribution to formative assessment

Factual account of what happened written by the learner
On 20 September we made Spaghetti Bolognaise, using mince, fresh tomatoes, onions, garlic.
Students from the next door class came in at the end and all had a taste
Indicates level of activity attempted and may indicate level of success.

Reflection on the learning experience by the learner.
I like garlic so I used a lot of it but the people who tried it said they liked it but were worried their breath would smell, so I will need to take account of that next time I make Bolognaise. I stuck closely to the recipe and the sauce was less runny than I usually make it.
Indicates how learner has learned from the previous experience and has indicated how s/he will improve as a result of this experience.

Comment by tutor
This really was one of your best dishes yet. Your decision to be stricter with yourself about use of the recipe really paid off. I would not worry too much about the garlic complaints, people should expect it in Italian cookery!
Offers tutor authentication to student's own view of what happened

Peer Comment
I did like your 'Spag Bol' – For once I think yours was better than mine!
A bit of Parmesan would have just finished it off though
Fellow student offering support but also offering suggestions for future action.

Quiz software for formative assessment and feedback

Quiz software can be used to create and administer formative assessments. These can be short multiple-choice type questions where learners test their understanding of the course so far. The quizzes can be retaken until the learner gets full marks. Longer 'free text' answers can also be used.

After the first three weeks of an introduction to IT course an online quiz can be used for learners to judge their own progress.

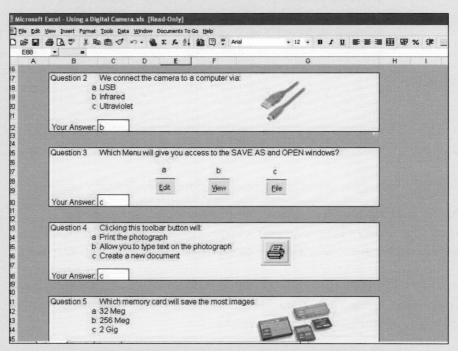

Example of quiz administered as part of a formative assessment by Luton Adult Education Service

Recording progress in oral skills

Using an audio recorder, performance in oral language skills can be captured at several points within a course and progress monitored. The audio files can then be collected together and made available through a PC or other devices. Sound quality is less crucial than ease of portability of the recorded files.

Spanish class

In a beginner's class learners worked in pairs to make voice recordings on an MP3 player of key phrases learned each week. Initially, headsets were used for playback to keep noise levels down in the classroom and to make the experience less 'public'. At the mid-term review the partners listened back to each other's recordings and used a paper form to comment on their own and their partner's progress. The tutor then verified the result and made final comments on the form.

RARPA Stage 5:
End-of-programme learner self-assessment; tutor summative assessment; review of overall progress and achievement.

The final stage of the RARPA process is assessment in relation to the learning objectives identified at the beginning and during the programme. It may include recognition of learning outcomes not specified during the programme.

Assessment at the end of a period of study will give a learner a final indication of the achievement during the course. The assessment should test the achievement of the course aims and the agreed individual objectives.

It should allow the learner and tutor to identify clearly the 'distance travelled' by the learner during the course.

A useful component of a summative assessment can be a test, which allows for comparison with answers given as part of the initial assessment. This is something which can be easily done with some of the quiz software, which stores and analyses the results of individual learners.

Digital devices are particularly good at capturing 'final artefacts' of learning. These can include photographs of physical products (meals cooked, ceramics made) and audio products (a guitar tune played, or a dialogue in a foreign language).

Audio recording of musical skills

An audio recorder can be powerful tool to capture and play back musical performances. The quality of the recording is more important with music than with voice recording. The facility to play back the recording immediately to the learner can also increase the value of this method.

Guitar playing

A learner joined a beginner's guitar playing course and did not have much confidence in his ability to learn to play the guitar.

The tutor for the course wanted her learners to be able to recognise and realise how much their guitar playing can improve in a six-week course. To do this she made use of a mini-disc recorder and every week recorded short clips of each learner playing the guitar.

The learner listened to these clips individually with his tutor and heard for himself the improvements in his guitar playing. The recordings also gave the tutor an opportunity to discuss with the learner any improvements that could be made. At the end of the course, the tutor played back the recording of all the previous weeks to the learner so that he could hear for himself his achievement.

Quiz for summative assessment

A carefully prepared quiz can be a very useful way of demonstrating that learning objectives have been achieved. Where class members have negotiated individual learning objectives this should be reflected in the quiz questions they are asked to answer.

Cycle maintenance quiz

At the end of a cycle maintenance course, all learners undertook a multiple choice quiz set on the learning platform. The quiz had at least one question for each of the course learning objectives. There was a free text box at the end of the quiz for learners to add anything else they thought they had learned from the course.

The results were printed out and given to learners in a plastic wallet as evidence of their achievement on the course.

Showcasing learners' work

A provider's website or a learner's e-portfolio can be used to showcase and present final pieces of work in art, crafts, photography and creative writing.

Art online in Cornwall

On the Cornwall art online website, the art students put up images of their work at the end of a course with the option to add their own thoughts on their achievements. This provides a platform for learners to share their achievements with friends and family who can view the website from anywhere in the world and gives learners a great sense of achievement in having their work published on the Internet.

Painting

5 sub-albums and no images in this album

[slideshow] [login]

Gallery: Cornwall Art Online ⇧

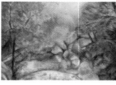

Album: Abstract

Contains: 13 items.

Album: Landscape

Contains: 10 items.

Album: Portrait

Contains: 23 items.

Album: Seascape

Contains: 24 items.

Album: Still Life

Contains: 14 items.

Gallery: Cornwall Art Online ⇧

Powered by Gallery v1.4.3-pl2

home | gallery | links | artists | email us | help

screenshot from Cornwall art online

Video record of final performances

In areas of the performing arts, an important test of the success of the learning will be the contribution of individuals to a final performance. These events have great potential for both testing of skills gained and celebrating success. A video can be very valuable, especially when the approach to the filming takes account of the need to recognise achievements of individuals and the whole class.received copies of the video to take home with them and were asked to give permission for their tutor to use the video during the local adult learners week celebrations.

Belly-dancing show

The final assessment of achievement in a belly-dancing class was a planned performance on the last session of the term. Five minutes of the performance were videoed. The camera operator ensured that she had some close up footage of each learner.

After the performance, each learner spoke to camera about what she gained by attending the course and reflecting on whether she had learned anything that that she had not expected to learn. Windows Moviemaker software was used to add captions to the final video naming each learner. The learners then received copies of the video to take home with them and were asked to give permission for their tutor to use the video during the local Adult Learners Week celebrations.

3 **Planning to use technology**

The previous chapter showed how a number of technologies are available to record learner progress and achievement. This chapter will give an outline of some of the broad issues which teachers need to consider before adopting a digital method to the RARPA process. Following this, chapters 4, 5, 6 and 7 look in greater detail at the operational considerations for specific types of hardware and software. In a world of rapidly-evolving technology and with innovative practitioners always seeking new ways to integrate technology in their teaching and learning, we can expect new software and new devices to be added to the list all the time.

As e-learning becomes adopted more widely in the delivery of learning materials and activities so technology is becoming an increasingly popular approach to recording learner progress and achievement in a non-bureaucratic way. However, there are a number of questions, which need to be considered before decisions are made about using particular technologies to record learner progress and achievement.

The purpose of the technology

Here are some questions to address before embarking on a use of technology to record progress and achievement:

- What is being recorded and for what purpose?
- How will the recording be used and by whom?
- What is the advantage to be gained through using technology to undertake the identified task(s)?

If you are unable to provide convincing answers to these questions then you need to consider whether the use of technology is really necessary or useful to your learners.

Usability

The technology used to record progress and achievement needs to be easy to use for both the learners and the tutors. If the learners and tutors have difficulty understanding the technology then they are less likely to engage with it. Also if you find that the majority of the lesson is spent familiarising yourself and your learners with the new technology or spent dealing with technical problems then, again, you need to think about whether the benefits of that particular technology are worth the time and effort.

Accessibility

It is important to ask whether the use of the technology excludes certain users. When a disability means that a learner will not be able to use a particular method then reasonable adjustments or equivalent alternatives must be made available. For public providers it is important that the application of any process to record progress complies with the organisation's Disability Equality Scheme.

Availability of the technology

The venue where you deliver the course may influence the type of technology that you are able to use with your learners. Some technology may require additional equipment in order to maximise its impact on the learner. For example, if you are using digital cameras in the classroom, then it is useful to be able to show the learner the image on a laptop or PC, as the camera screens are often too small to make out any detail. Similarly, playing back video clips is a lot clearer on a monitor or laptop than on the camera screen.

Some of the quiz software will also benefit from having a data projector and interactive whiteboard.

Learners' permissions

Some learners may not be comfortable with having their voices recorded or having their images taken. It is important that the learners are made aware of exactly how any material collected will be used and who will have access to it. Ownership of the materials collected should ideally lie with the learners and it is important that permissions about any recordings are agreed at the start of the course.

Managing the data recorded

It is important to have a system in place to catalogue, store and retrieve the material recorded. The issue of where the data and recordings will be stored needs to be addressed. For example, will each learner have his or her own 'learning space' on a learning platform or network, or will the learner's work be stored locally on one machine or an external hard drive?

You will also need to think about the security of the data that is collected and consider these questions:

- Will the records be password-protected?
- Will other people be given access to the learner's work?
- How will the work be accessed?

Training

There needs to be adequate time to train tutors to use any new technology. Many tutors work on a part-time or sessional basis which can make it difficult to co-ordinate training schedules. The training needs to cover not only how to use the technology, but also how to integrate it into the teaching and learning context. Time and resources should be allocated for additional one-to-one support that may be required by individual tutors when first using the equipment in their classes.

Cost of implementing and using technology

The cost of using the technology is not just the purchase cost, but also includes any maintenance costs, additional software which you may require, depreciation and replacement costs and paying for training and technician time.

4 Digital devices for sight and sound

This chapter will consider some of the hand-held devices which can be used in classes to capture evidence in visual or audio form. It deals with some of the practical issues associated with deploying these devices in a teaching situation.

Digital photographs

Digital cameras are an obvious choice to capture images of learners' work or to show the learners themselves in the process of learning. The wide-ranging choice of digital cameras available on the market means that tutors and organisations can often find one that suits their budget and needs.

Many tutors and learners are familiar with use of digital cameras to take images. To gain full benefit from digital images there are additional skills that must be acquired such as transferring images to a PC, uploading information to websites, image manipulation and file-naming.

Using a digital camera

Other devices such as Personal Digital Assistants (PDAs), mobile phones and integrated voice/image recorders can also be used to take still images, but often with a lower resolution (lower quality) than a digital camera. If the quality of the image is not of importance and budgets are limited, then some of these devices could be a useful alternative to using a digital camera.

Photo-printers are also becoming increasingly popular with tutors as they allow them to print directly from the digital camera without the need for a PC or laptop. This can be particularly useful for tutors who deliver lessons in centres where there is no access to a PC or laptop or for tutors who do not feel they have the skills and time necessary to transfer the images from a digital camera onto a computer.

A photo printer will allow you to view and print an image without the use of a PC or laptop

The viewing of an image or set of images by a learner can produce some powerful narratives on the progress of the course or reflection on the learning process. There is great value in integrating image collection with text and audio evidence from learners.

Tips for using cameras in the classroom

Battery life

Charge the camera before taking it to the lesson or if it requires batteries then always carry a spare set with you.

Storage space on the device

Make sure that the memory card in the camera has the capacity to store all the images you need. Delete or transfer existing images on the camera to create more space for new images, or buy a larger size of memory card if you think you will be taking a large number of images during your course.

Permission

Ensure that learners have signed permission forms before you take any images of them or their work (See Appendix 1). This is equally important for any other type of recording device you may use, for example recording learners' voices or filming in the classroom.

Viewing images

If you want to show the images to the learners during the lesson then you will need a laptop/PC, USB cable or card reader to upload the images onto, or a photo printer to print the images directly. A lot of the digital cameras come with a viewer screen, but some learners may find it difficult to see the images clearly on the small screen.

Image storage

Most cameras take photographs of good quality (high resolution), which are large file sizes (over 1 Megabyte sometimes). Whilst the images are good, the pictures are often too large to e-mail, to place on a website or learning platform. Possible solutions include:

● Compressing the images using software (e.g. Photoshop Elements, Gimp and Picassa)
● Some websites will reduce the size of the displayed image automatically
● Some cameras offer low-resolution (or e-mail) versions of images.

Before capturing images make sure you have tested the route to the final destination!

File names

Cameras usually give images sequential numbers. It may be useful to change these numbers to names, when you transfer the images to your PC/laptop. Use a format that is meaningful to your group e.g.
SC0000876 may be renamed to show the learner name, date and the title of the course: **GJones-2May06-WaterC**

For more information see NIACE's e-guideline 2, *Digital cameras in teaching and learning.*

Digital video

Digital video camcorders make video recordings in digital format. They save the files on tape or other medium such as recordable DVD or internal hard drive and are useful tools for recording learner progress and achievement. Like audio recorders, they can be used to capture spoken statements by learners, but the video element can provide the additional non-verbal information conveyed by body language, including facial expressions and gestures. However, in areas of physical skill such as sports and fitness a video record can be particularly valuable in recording movements.

Using a digital camcorder

The cost of digital camcorders can sometimes be prohibitive for providers. However, many digital 'still' cameras, as well as PDAs and other small hand-held devices, can also take short video clips, which may be adequate for making a swift short record of a stage in the learning process.

Digital camcorders can be a really useful tool to record learners' movements in a dance or fitness class and then played back to them so that the learner can see for themselves how well they are doing or to see ways in which they can improve their technique in dancing or fitness.

Some tutors who use camcorders in their lessons find that they are then not able to devote sufficient time to actual teaching as they are too busy recording the learners! This can be overcome by using a volunteer or assistant to do the recording or to involve learners in recording each other. However, the assistant would need some training in using the digital camcorder and to be briefed on what aspects of the lesson they should be recording.

Some learners may feel uncomfortable about being filmed. Tutors should be aware of this and ensure that learners give permission for themselves to be filmed and to understand how the material will be used.

Tips for using video cameras in the classroom

Preparation

Before the lesson, check that the camera is fully charged or that it can be plugged safely to a mains power plug point and that you carry spare DV tapes or blank DVDs.

Editing

If you want to edit any of the video footage on a PC, then make sure your PC has a fast enough processor and plenty of memory (RAM), or else you could be spending hours editing a five-minute clip! You also need a video editing card and software, although Microsoft Windows XP now comes bundled with Moviemaker, which is a useful basic video editing package.

If you are editing using an Apple iMAC then this comes with a video editing package (iMovie) and Firewire sockets which allow you to connect your camcorder directly to the computer.

Tripod

A tripod will help to keep the camera steady and allow the camera to be set up in one position whilst the tutor can carry on with teaching.

Storage

If the purpose of the video clip is to provide immediate feedback to a learner, then the clip can be deleted after the learner has seen it and there is no need to store it. If the recording is to gather evidence of progression or achievement or is a performance as part of a summative assessment, then tutors need to give some consideration as to where and how the recording will be stored, as most video clips can take up a lot of storage space on a hard drive. Possible solutions include:

- Saving short video clips on an external hard drive freeing up space on your PC but still allowing you to view them from any computer with a media player.
- If the video clips do not need editing then you can store and view them directly from the DV tape (you will need an AV cable to connect the camcorder to a TV, monitor or data projector).
- If the video clip is evidence of a learner's piece of work, e.g. a dance routine, then it can be saved to CD-ROM or DVD, which the learner can also have a copy of to take home with them. With the CD-ROM you will need to compress the file, which will result in some loss of quality. Also, once a file has been compressed, it will be difficult to do any further editing with it.

Microphones

If you are recording conversations/interviews using a camcorder, then consider using an external microphone to ensure high quality sound.

Audio recordings

Audio recording can take place using various technologies such as MP3 players/recorders, dictaphones, talking sticks, minidisk recorders, or the audio recording function on PDAs and mobile phones.

Audio recorders can be relatively inexpensive and often less intrusive to use with learners than cameras and camcorders.

Audio recorders can be particularly useful for recording discussions and conversations with learners about their personal goals and the progress they are making towards the goals.

Using audio recorders can also be a useful way for modern foreign language or ESOL learners to record examples of their own progress in learning a new language and to improve their pronunciation by listening back to their recordings.

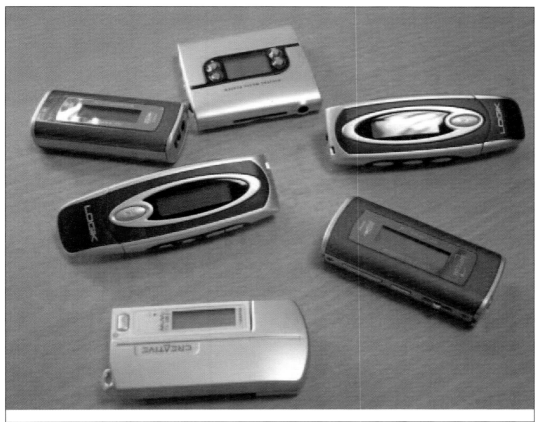

A variety of audio recorders

Tips on using audio recorders in a classroom

Formats

Some audio recorders use formats (e.g. wav) which can easily be transferred to a PC. However, others use a format specific to the manufacturer. This may be fine if you only ever intend to play back through the recording device but may require conversion software if used on a PC.

Naming files

Audio files will normally have a numerical file name. However some of the devices will allow you to name the files on the device to something more meaningful such as:

0009876.wav to Assif-10may05pots.wav
(student name – date – class)

Some of the more expensive models will even allow you to create folders on the device so that you can file and manage the recordings done by individual learners.

Sound quality

Audio recorders are designed to be adequate to record speech but they do vary in sound quality and some may not be adequate where sound quality needs to be high e.g. music or singing. The quality of the recording may be low, especially with some of the smaller MP3 devices, which will pick up a lot of background noise and make it difficult to hear conversations.

Storage space

Audio files can take up a lot of storage space and if you are going to be using the files in each lesson, for example to play back to learners what they had done in the previous session, then it may be useful saving the files onto a removable storage device such as an external hard drive. If you decide to store and play the files from the audio device then make sure you still back these up on a hard drive. Some of the smaller devices are not very robust and any damage to the device could result in the loss of data.

Personal digital assistants

Personal digital assistants (PDAs) are small lightweight electronic hand-held devices that can be used in a variety of ways to capture a learner's progress. Most PDAs can be used as a combined camera, camcorder and voice recorder, although the quality of the recordings on the PDA will be limited. PDAs come with a stylus, which can be used to write on the screen or a full-size keyboard is also available for most models which folds down to the size of the PDA itself, making it easier to type and navigate around the PDA. PDAs can also communicate with your desktop computer, allowing you to transfer data easily and quickly from the computer to the PDA and vice-versa. Data can be transferred to and from the PDA in several ways:

● The expansion memory card can be removed and placed in a card reader that is connected to a PC.
● A wireless connection (blue tooth or infra red) can be made with a PC.
● A synchronisation cable can be connected to a PC.

One advantage that PDAs have over the other recording technologies is the capability to name files as soon as they are recorded rather than to have to download them onto a PC or laptop before they can be given a meaningful name.

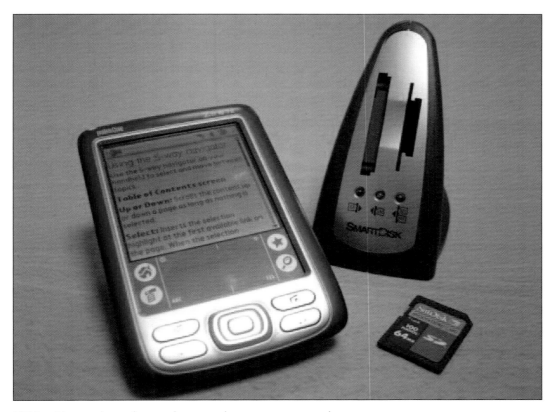

PDA with card reader and expansion memory card.

Tips on using PDAs in the classroom

Synchronising with a PC

PDAs are designed for a single device to synchronise with a single PC. If you are using a number of devices with a class you may wish to download data for all the devices to one machine. To do this you need to give each PDA an individual name so that the data from each device will only synchronise to the corresponding folder on the PC. Some practitioners have found it easier to save data to a memory card of a PDA and then remove the card and transfer data via a card reader.

Battery life

It is advisable to charge the PDAs before the lesson. If you are using multiple handsets with your learners, then you can buy storage boxes that allow all the handsets to be charged with just one plug.

Familiarisation sessions

PDAs may seem like complicated pieces of technologies with various buttons and functions. But a brief 20-minute session familiarising learner with the various functions is probably all that is required. Most learners who have used other digital recording devices or mobile phone will find it fairly easy to transfer their knowledge to using a PDA.

5 Tools for asking questions

There is a variety of software which can be used to create online quizzes and tests. Many learning platforms also contain their own quiz tools. Online quizzes, tests and self-assessment questionnaires can all play a key part in initial, formative and summative assessments. This chapter explores some of the practical issues for tutors who plan to use these resources.

Online quiz tools

The most straightforward use for quiz tools is to set quizzes which offer a set of answers from which to select, either as multiple choice or some form of matching correct answers. Careful choice of the 'distractors' (incorrect options in multiple choice) is very important to avoid correct answers being too obvious. Online quiz tools offer a number of useful functions:

- A learner can make several attempts at a quiz and the results can be stored on a database and compared to see whether the learners' scores and understanding of a subject have improved.
- Time taken on a quiz can be recorded. This can highlight questions where the learner is taking longer to respond.
- Feedback can be provided immediately to the learner.
- Questions from previous tests can be reassembled into new quizzes to re-test areas identified for additional coverage.
- Test scores can be compiled into a learner's portfolio.

Tips on using quiz tools

Question design

In designing multiple-choice questions consider these tips:

● The stem or question should be worded simply and involve one issue only.
● The answer to one question should not be obtainable from another question.
● The distractors (incorrect options) should be brief and as homogeneous as possible.

Adult & Community Learning

Family Learning

8. Which of the following is an example of alliteration?
   • boom, bang, crash, wallop!
   • Richard of York goes battling in vain.
   • ripe, red raspberries

9. How many syllables has the word "super"
   • 2
   • 5
   • 3

An initial assessment quiz used with a Family Learning
writing class in Sheffield

● The distractors should be plausible (eg mistakes often made by students).
● Take care not to have a pattern for the position of the correct response.

Validity of results

Lucky guessing in multiple choice questions can lead to skewed results but this can be minimised with careful choice of questions and 'distractors'.

Most online quiz tools allow you to offer feedback to users for each question. This feedback can be as simple as just 'right' or 'wrong'. However imaginative use of the feedback fields can transform a formative test into a learning experience.

Free text answers

For some questions use of free text answers is appropriate (for example to test spelling ability). It is important that all acceptable version of the correct answer are provided.

Online self-assessment tools

Self-assessment can play a very important part in encouraging learners to judge their own position in a learning process. Software tools exist with pre-prepared self-assessment questions, but in many situations tutors will want to customise their own self-assessment questions.

At a very simple level an assessment could be based on an interactive Microsoft Word document with drop-down menu offering options. The resulting document can be dated and printed or saved electronically.

An example of a self assessment created in Microsoft Word using drop down boxes.

Some, but not all, online quiz creation software is also suitable for setting self-assessment questionnaires. It is also possible to set questions and save answers to a database so that results from the same set of self-assessment question can be compared during a course.

Tips on using electronic self assessment

Mediation

Self-assessment results will almost certainly raise questions with learners, which should be discussed with the tutor. It is important to make sure that after taking a self-assessment the learner can progress swiftly to a dialogue with the tutor about his/her learning needs.

Confirmation

There may be value in linking objective tests to self-assessment in order to confirm the learner's own judgement. Some software allows transfer from a self-assessment to an objective test question to confirm.

Writing descriptors

The descriptors need to be written very clearly to ensure that there is no ambiguity.

Space for free text

Even where most questions may have multiple choice answers it is important to include space for additional information or explanation from the learner through a free text box or the option to offer oral explanation of answers given.

File names

If using an interactive Word document it is important to change the file name of the individual learner's record before saving, to avoid it being over-written.

E.g. the blank form for a Keep Fit class may have the file name **KF-SAssess.doc**

The learner's may be saved as:
BillBaileyKF-SAssess.doc

Interactive voting software

Quizzes or multiple choice questions are simple techniques which many tutors have been using for years to assess a learner's starting point or their understanding of a subject at the end- or mid-point through a course. The only difference now is that many of these quizzes and multiple-choice questions can be made more interactive and more suited to different learning styles by using various software and new technology.

Interactive voting systems or Classroom Performance Systems consist of handsets which are linked to a PC or laptop through a wireless system. Questions can be projected onto a screen or whiteboard where the learners view them. The buttons on the individual handsets are used to vote or indicate their responses to the questions.

The tutors can develop questionnaires that are specific to the course to assess prior knowledge and the progress made by the learners. The questionnaires can contain both words and images, and can be customised with colour, different font types and character sizes. The questionnaires can potentially be used for different learning styles and take into account individual learner needs to make the process of assessment more "fun". These questionnaires can often engage learners who would normally be put off by paper-based assessments.

Learners can respond anonymously and will not feel the pressure of getting a question wrong in front of their peers. Also the results can be available immediately and used to engage the group in discussion about their learning goals.

Tutors may find that they need to spend some time developing the questions to use for the quiz. However, the voting software will analyse the responses of individual learners which means that tutors do not have to spend any time marking the responses at the end of the quiz. The analysis of the questions will also highlight areas which are proving most challenging. This enables the tutor to plan which areas of the course to concentrate on for the next session. The results of any quiz or assessments can also be stored on the database, so a tutor can check on a learner's progress over the duration of the course.

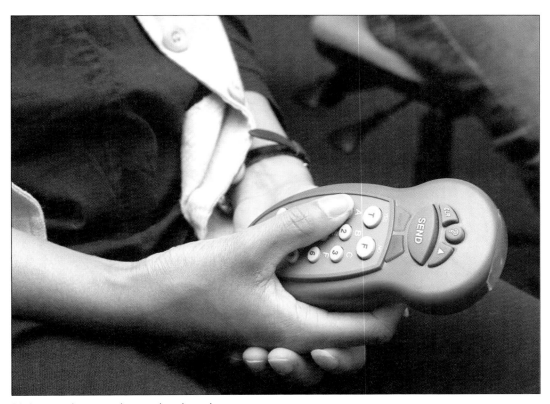

Using an interactive voting handset

Tips on using interactive voting systems in the classroom

- The system will require peripherals such as a laptop and a data projector to work effectively.
- Tutors should be given the opportunity to take the equipment away and experiment with ways in which they could use the quiz software with their own classes.
- The tutor preparing the quiz will need to have access to this software in advance, either on the presentation PC or installed on another machine that is more accessible to him/her.
- Handsets need to contain charged batteries. Learners do not take kindly to being disenfranchised because of exhausted batteries!
- Where individual learners' scores are being tracked, the tutor should note the learners' names against handset numbers.
- The interactive voting system could be adapted to suit the needs of learners with different learning styles by altering the way in which the questions are presented or making use of images or audio. Learners with difficulties in reading from the whiteboard can be given a printed copy of the questions but still use the voting pad to record their responses.

What learners in Doncaster said about using about voting handsets

"I think that using the handsets is a good idea because it helps to identify the needs of the class."

"They are easy to use, better than a form to fill in."

"It shows we have learnt something from the beginning to the end of class."

6 Digital learning spaces

Digital learning spaces are virtual spaces which learners can access online to store, organise, and reflect on their work. They can also provide a way of showcasing and celebrating the products of learning. This chapter looks at some of the types of digital learning space and considers how tutors can use these effectively.

Blogs

Blogs or weblogs can be described as an online space which learners use to keep a journal or reflective log of their learning. Blogs can be stand-alone online tools or may be incorporated in a learning platform (see page 37) or e-portfolio (see page 38). Through careful phrasing of key questions by the tutor, a blog can provide a powerful tool for recording achievement.

A blog can include:
- the product of learning (e.g. the writing in English or target language to be learned can be the evidence of written language ability)
- a factual account of what happened
- a reflection on the learning experience
- tutor comments
- peer comments

Tips on using blogs

- The choice of blog software or platform will depend on a number of factors such as
- How easy is it to use for the learners?
- What functions do you require from a blog? For example, will learners be uploading images, video clips or audio to their blogs?
- What sort of budget do you have to set up the blogs for your learners? There are a number of free services, but they will be limited in terms of functionality and storage capacity – but some of the free services may be sufficient for the needs of your class.

Most 'blog' software allows users to choose who can read the blog.
The options can include
- only the writer
- the writer and tutor
- the writer, tutor and class
- anyone using the net

Putting this control in the hands of the learners is an important part of ensuring that they have confidence to contribute and have a sense of ownership.

Blogs can be configured to allow comments from other group members or even external viewers. This function should be negotiated with learners and a group policy agreed for writing of comments.

Many blog applications or platforms offer free trial versions, which often have reduced features. It is worth trying the free versions before committing to using a particular blogging tool.

daclarts1

Artwork by N Devon ACL students. To comment: click Login, type 'guest' & 'pigment', click Login then 'View site'

« After Rembrandt 2 - Acrylic
Alice Liddell - watercolour »

Autumn study - Ink & watercolour

A small study of autumn leaves and fruit showing good colour range to suggest form and tone.

This entry was posted on Friday, February 17th, 2006 at 9:53 am and is filed under General, Still Life. You can follow any responses to this entry through the RSS 2.0 feed. You can skip to the end and leave a response. Pinging is currently not allowed.

One Response to "Autumn study - Ink & watercolour"

1. *Tony* Says:
   March 14th, 2006 at 8:46 pm

   A very good impression of one of our class specimens which is a bit past its paint by date. The choice of colours and shades are just right and the style free and flowing.

Leave a Reply

You must be logged in to post a comment.

daclarts1 - **Powered by** WordPress
Entries (RSS) **and** Comments (RSS).

A blog used in a still life class in Devon, with learner and tutor comments.

Learning platforms

A learning platform offers an online location where a learner's electronic learning resources can be accessed and organised. They are sometimes known by other names, such as Virtual Learning Environments (VLEs) or Learning Management Systems (LMS). By integrating the activity in one 'platform' it is possible to collect diverse evidence of an individual's contribution and progression. For example, it is usually possible to group together an individual's contributions to all of the discussion forums. It is possible to track quiz scores, time taken and number of attempts. Platforms often allow the creation of collaborative work such as Wikis, but will still make it possible to identify the contribution made by each individual. By encouraging access to the platform between sessions the tutors can set assessment tasks between meetings and the results can then be used to help to plan future sessions.

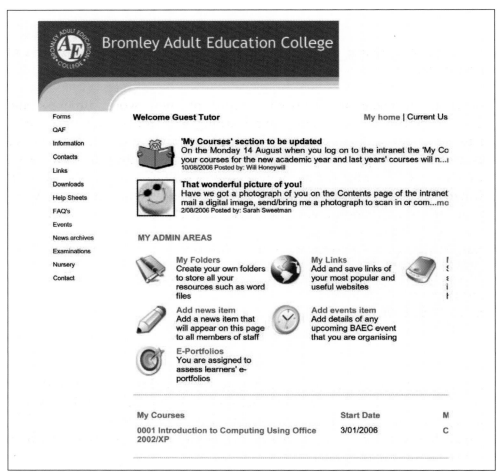

Example of a learning platform

Tips for recording progress and achievement using a learning platform

Potential complexity

Platforms can offer a great deal of sophisticated functionality which can be overwhelming to part-time learners so it is important to make careful choices about which functions will fit usefully within your learning programme.

Staff development

It is important that staff have received some training and guidance on how to use a learning platform. Tutors who use the learning platform for their own training and learning are more likely to be confident about using the learning platform with their learners.

E-portfolios

One way of drawing together evidence of progress and achievement is in the creation of individual e-portfolios for learners.

E-portfolios allow learners to make an electronic record of their work, progress and achievements as well as to reflect on and share their learning with others. There is much debate as to what a typical e-portfolio should look like and contain. Some e-portfolios are online storage spaces accessed through special software (as in Higher Education). However, other tools can be used as an e-portfolio, for example: learning platforms, a CD-ROM, USB Memory Stick, dedicated webspace, or even a shared folder on an internal network. An e-portfolio will largely be defined by its purpose, contents and user group.

An e-portfolio will generally support one or more of these functions:

- Electronic scrapbook
- Individual Learning Plan
- Recording progress and achievement
- Assessment
- Showcasing

An e-portfolio is linked to a particular individual but may be intended to be viewed by a range of other people including peers, teachers, external verifiers, potential employers, and admissions staff from another educational institution. In addition, the owner of the e-portfolio could make content available to others such as friends and family or, by publishing with an open web address, to anyone surfing the web.

Making the whole contents of an e-portfolio freely available via the web could expose learners to the risk of their personal details, including images and personal reflections, being accessed by third parties. Security of data belonging to adults needs to be a joint responsibility, with educational providers offering clear information and the owner of the data taking the ultimate decision.

E-portfolio

Audience for content	Reasons to use E-portfolio	Examples of content
The learner	Contribute content as a record of learning. ● Reflective learning log ● Products of learning ● Evidence of achievement	● Reflective learning log ● 'work in progress' ● completed assignments ● Evidence of skills progression
The learner's peers	To learn from the reflections of other learners. To offer and receive peer support through making comments on the learning log. To view examples of achievements.	● Reflective learning log ● Examples of work produced
The teacher/tutor	Monitor progress of learner through a learning log. Collect assignments and other work for assessment. Contribute comments to the portfolio.	Learning log ● Initial assessments ● Documentation of agreed learning goals ● Formative assessments
External verifiers	1) Summative assessment, course work 2) Evidence of quality learning processes (e.g. RARPA)	● Summative assessment ● Course work ● Evidence of process
Potential employers/ admissions staff from an educational institution	CV including list of formal qualifications. Examples of 'showcase' work.	● CV ● formal qualifications ● 'Showcase' work
Others	This could include the celebration of the success of family members or friends.	All of the above evidence could be presented.

7 **Making it happen**

This book has highlighted a number of approaches to using technology to record learner progress and achievement. Tutors from across the country have used these technologies in some very creative ways to engage their learners and to help them to recognise for themselves the progress and achievements they have made in their learning.

It is worth noting that the examples illustrated in this book were dependent on the tutor being provided with training and support. Staff training and ongoing support is key to the effective use of the technology with the learners.

Digital technology allows for the collection and use of a very rich and diverse range of evidence. This evidence can have very powerful emotional associations for the learners. For this reason the material should been seen as the property of the learner and he or she should always be in control of the ways that it is presented to others.

Finally, any approach to recording learner progress and achievement needs to be fit for purpose and appropriate for your group of learners. Digital technology should be used to make the process of target-setting and recording achievement more meaningful to the learner. It should not become an additional burden or hinder the learning process.

References

Books

Greenwood, M and Wilson, P (2004) *Recognising and Recording progress and achievement in non-accredited learning – Evaluation Report on the RARPA pilot projects April 2003-March 2004*, NIACE and LSDA

Hardcastle, P (2004) *Digital cameras in teaching and learning*, NIACE

Luger, E (2006) – *The Potential of E learning, 2005* (Available from ICT team, NIACE)

LSC (2005) *RARPA For Action Document.*

Minschull, G and Powell, B (2004) *Choosing and using a learning platform in ACL* (Available from ICT team, NIACE)

Useful Resources

RARPA
Greenwood, M & Wilson, P. (2004) RARPA *Evaluation report on the RARPA*, NIACE

LSC Effective Practice website
www.lsc.gov.uk/rarpa
Information about RARPA and links to the RARPA Effective Practice Web Resource (EPWR)

E-Learning in Adult and Community Learning
www.aclearn.net
Information about the learning outcomes projects who participated who piloted the use of technology for RARPA

Staff development in e-learning

Community learning resource
www.aclearn.net

Staff development e-learning centre
www.aclearn.net/sdelc

Learning and Skills Web
www.learningandskillsweb.org.uk

Accessibility

Useful resources and advice on accessible technology to use with learners
http://www.techdis.ac.uk
http://www.abilitynet.co.uk

Learning platforms

Information on popular open source platform
http://www.moodle.org

Adoption of learning platforms in adult learning
http://www.aclearn.net/platform1

Quizzes

Many learning platforms contain tools for quiz creation. In addition there are some stand-alone options – these are just are two examples:

Hot Potatoes: **http://hotpot.uvic.ca/**
Question Tools: **http://www.questiontools.co.uk/**

Online Survey tools

Quia: **http://www.guia.com**
Survey Monkey: **http://surveymonkey.com**

Interactive voting systems

There are several companies offering this technology. Here are just two examples:

Quizdom: **http://www.qwizdom.co.uk/**
Activote: **http://www.prometheanworld.com/uk/activote**

Digital cameras and images

PICASA
Free software from Google which can be used to edit and organise digital images.
http://picasa.google.co.uk/

GIMP
Freely-distributed software for such tasks as photo retouching and image retouching.
http://www.gimp.org/

Adobe Photoshop – commercially available photo software.
http://www.adobe.com/products/photoshop/

Digital audio

Audacity
Free, open-source software for recording and editing sound.
http://audacity.sourceforge.net/

Glossary

Blog – 'A weblog' an online journal consisting of links and entries in chronological order.

CD – A compact disc. This can be used to store computer data.

Compression – In relation to digital files this term refers to the process of reducing the size of a file by compressing the data. This compression can lead to easier file management but it will involve some loss of quality.

Disability Equality Scheme – as part of their Disability Equality Duty, public bodies are required to prepare a Disability Equality Scheme which commits them to act proactively to meet the needs of disabled people.

ESOL – English for Speakers of Other Languages.

E-portfolio – E-portfolios are digital storage spaces (often online) which allow learners to make an electronic record of their work, progress and achievements. There is a variety of approaches to e-portfolio design depending on the intended audience for the material and the type of study followed.

Firewire – a high speed cabling technology for connecting computers to high capacity storage devices, for example digital camcorders.

Flash drive – A computer memory data storage device usually about the size of a packet of chewing gum which can be connected to a computer using the USB port.

Hot Potatoes – A software system which can be used to produce online quizzes.

Interactive voting systems – A system which uses wireless connected handsets to allow all learners in a class to respond to questions displayed on a whiteboard.

Learning management system – See Learning Platform.

Learning platform – Offers an online location where a learner's electronic learning resources can be accessed and organised. Sometimes known by other names such as Virtual Learning Environments (VLEs) or Learning Management Systems (LMS).

Memory Expansion Card – small card that can be inserted into handheld devices to increase memory capacity.

Memory Stick – see Flash drive.

MPEG (Moving Picture Experts Group) – The term refers to the family of digital video compression standards and file formats developed by the group. MPEG files can be decoded by special hardware or by software.

MP3 (MPEG Audio Layer 3) –a common file format for music and other audio content. It is commonly used on the Internet, on PCs, and on portable devices, including dedicated music players and phones with music player functionality.

Personal Digital Assistant (PDA) – a hand-held electronic device which can include some of the functionality of a computer, a cellphone, a music player and a camera.

Questiontools – A software tool which can be used to create online quizzes.

RAM (Random Access Memory) – This memory is used by the computer while it is operating. The memory is very quick to access but all data is lost when the machine is closed down.

Resolution – In relation to digital images this refers to the quality of digital data used to create the image. A high-resolution image will offer a good quality picture, but may require a large amount of memory space.

Synchronisation Cable – Cable used to connect a hand held device to a PC in order to transfer data between the two.

USB (Universal Serial Bus) – This is a small device which allows other devices to be connected to your computer without the need for an adapter card. Most recent PCs have at least one port which will accept a USB cable.

VLE (Virtual Learning Environment) – See Learning Platform.

Wiki – a resource which allows users to collaborate on the creation and editing of a document online.

WMA (Windows Media Audio) – A Microsoft file format for encoding digital audio files similar to MP3 though it can compress files at a higher rate than MP3. WMA files, which use the '.wma' file extension, can be of any size and compressed to match many different connection speeds or bandwidths.

Appendix 1

Paper-free RARPA? A framework for discussion

This is a framework which can be used to explore possible paper-free approaches to applying RARPA. It is intended to be used after staff have had access to the examples of paper-free approaches to RARPA from this book and other sources.

The framework can be used to promote discussion with curriculum managers or with groups of tutors to explore approaches which they believe will work for their learners.

The framework can be used in a number of ways:

- It could be the basis of a time-limited online conference on the tutor section of your learning platform.

- It could be used to structure a half-day training session for curriculum staff.

- The framework could be transformed into a series of group or individual activities which could be delivered using digital technology.

- The framework could even be printed off and filled in as a paper form.

Current practice in applying **RARPA**	Possible paper-free approaches	Training/support required	Equipment/software required	Benefits	
	Option 1			for learner	
				for tutor	
	Option 2			for learner	
				for tutor	
	Option 3			for learner	
				for tutor	

Appendix 2

Example permission statement from learner

This is an example of statement which learners could be asked to sign to agree to the collection and storage of digital evidence.

I understand that recording my progress in this course will help me to recognise the progress I am making and it will assist my tutor to the plan the teaching sessions.

To support this I give my permission for a record of my progress to be made, on paper and in electronic format. I understand that the material is intended to be accessed by me and staff of the adult learning service. I understand that it may also be made available to external inspectors who are verifying the course processes. For any additional use of the material (e.g. publicity or staff training) I will be asked to give separate authorisation.

Learner's signature_____

Date _____

Appendix 3

List of providers who participated in the Technology and Learning Outcomes Pilot 2004–05

During 2004 and 2005, the LSC funded a number of projects through NIACE, to pilot the use of technology to implement RARPA. The experiences reported by these projects have contributed to this book.

Cheshire County Council

Using 3G cards for wireless internet access, megasticks for voice recording and data storage, and a classroom voting system with capabilities to record and analyse progress with up to 32 separate learner channels.

Doncaster Metropolitan Borough Council

Using infra-red [IR] remote control pads to engage learners in an initial and summative assessment process, focusing on two-hour taster sessions in basic IT, craft, and health and beauty courses.

Dudley Council

Using PDAs with ESOL learners to use as work scrapbooks, within which photographs, videos and sound clips collected by learners were held and organised.

Hull City Council Adult Education Services

The use of audio and video in recording learners' progression in three areas of Modern Foreign Languages – Spanish, French and Italian.

Peterborough Adult Learning Service

Using digital voice recorders to record learning outcomes for Swimming for Adults, Ballroom and Sequence Dancing, and Pottery.

Portsmouth City Council

Using a range of technology to improve initial and formative assessment in arts: using digital cameras and portable printers; Mimio whiteboard emulator; voice recorders; laptops and data projectors.

Reading Adult and Community College

Using digital cameras and video to record and assess learner progress mainly from visual and performing arts, and sports and fitness curriculum areas.

Sandwell Adult Education Service

Using video in craft-based subject areas, mainly Painting and Drawing, General Crafts and Pottery.

Wirral Lifelong Learning Services (MBC)

Using an initial assessment software for a series of three beginner IT courses.

Full reports on these projects are available on www.aclearn.net search on 'Learning outcomes'.

ABC SERIES

Another Cake Decorating Book

Contains many useful ideas for cake decoration

This book is dedicated to
Emily Jane Pitt,
my precious daughter and special friend.

D1322700

CONTENTS

	PAGE
Covering Cakes with Sugarpaste (Rolled Fondant)	2
Christening Robes	5
The Christmas Tree	6
Dancing Teddies Christening Cake & Daffodils	8
Cake Sides	11
Romantic Fruitful Drapes and Bows	13
Strawberry Fairies	19
Grapevine Frieze	22
The Teddy Bear's Picnic	24
Wild Rose Wedding Cake	28
Geometrical Designs for any Occasion	31
A Medley of Christmas Cards	32
Ideas for Cake Tops	36
Pram Christening Cake and Jasmine	43
Fantasy Cutwork Cake and Frangipani	46
RECIPES	27
Tylose Flower Paste	
Card Pastillage	
Tylose Glue / Petal Glue / Gum Glue	

All the tools and cutters referred to in this book are manufactured by

Jem Cutters cc

P.O. Box 115, Kloof, 3640 KwaZulu-Natal, South Africa

Tel: +27 (31) 701-1431   Fax: +27 (31) 701-0559   Email: jemcutters@iafrica.com

COVERING CAKES WITH SUGARPASTE
(ROLLED FONDANT)

The final covering of your cake depends upon the appearance of the cake itself.

CHECK LIST

1. Level the cake.
2. Turn the cake upside down.
3. Centre the cake on the cake board.
4. Boil smooth apricot jam to sterilise it.
5. Plug any small holes in the cake with pieces of marzipan.
6. Carefully cover cake with hot smooth apricot jam. Use a spatula or a pastry brush for this exercise.
7. Clean cake board of any surplus jam.
8. Sieve icing sugar on to a clean work top surface.
9. Roll out marzipan to desired thickness.
10. Use a piece of string as a guide to measure the diameter and sides of the cake to ensure you have sufficient marzipan.
11. Lift up marzipan either with a rolling pin, or use lifters.
12. Position marzipan over the top of the cake and allow to fall on to the middle of the cake
13. Smooth marzipan down using hands. Ensure that it reaches the base of the entire cake.
14. Make sure **no air** is trapped between the cake and the marzipan.
15. Cut off surplus marzipan with a knife.
16. Use smoothers to neaten the sides and top of the marzipan.
17. Clean cake board of any surplus icing sugar.
18. It is advisable to leave the cake to stand for at least a day or two to allow any oils to surface and dry out. Keep cake lightly covered with a clean cloth.

SUGARPASTE COVERING

- To prevent sugarpaste (rolled fondant) from cracking, it is important to knead the paste very well before rolling out. Avoid creating creases in the sugarpaste.
- Avoid incorporating air bubbles into the sugarpaste.
- If an air bubble does appear, use a sharp pin to allow the air to escape.
- Sieve icing sugar on to a clean work top surface
- Place sugarpaste in the middle of the icing sugar and using a rolling pin begin to flatten the fondant into the shape required for the cake. E.g. if you are covering a square cake, try to keep the fondant in a square shape.
- From time to time lift the fondant and turn it around to ensure it is not sticking.
- Polish the fondant with your hand in a circular motion.
- Roll out fondant to desired thickness. No less than 1 cm is recommended as if the fondant is too thin, it will stretch and break.
- Use a piece of string to measure the cake, the cake sides, and the cake board to ensure you have sufficient fondant.
- Wet the marzipan surface with a pastry brush. Use boiled water for this purpose.
- If you are covering the cake board as well, this should also be damp.
- Pick up the sugarpaste either with a rolling pin, or use lifters.
- Place the sugarpaste over the middle of the cake and remove the lifters or the roller causing the sugarpaste to fall into position on the cake.
- If you are covering a cake with corners, e.g. a square cake, work on the corners of the cake first, then the sides of the cake.
- When the cake appears smooth, use a pair of JEM Smoothers to smooth the top and the sides of your cake. This will create a professional appearance to the finish of the cake.
- Trim surplus sugarpaste using a knife or a pizza wheel.
- Ensure that the flat side of the smoothers is against the cake board.
- Avoid trapping any air between the cake and the sugarpaste. This could cause the sugarpaste to "blow".
- If an air bubble should appear in the fondant, use a sharp pin pressed into the fondant at an angle. Gently ease the air out of the bubble and hide the mark by rubbing a finger over it.
- Polish the covered cake using a clean smooth cloth. It is important to remove all traces of icing sugar.
- A well covered cake has no marks on it, and appears to have a polished surface.

ILLUSTRATIONS ON COVERING A CAKE

N.B. Read detailed instructions provided before you begin.

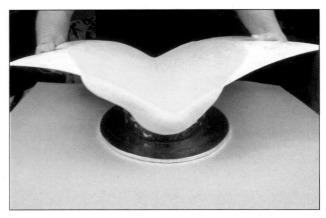

1 Plug the holes in the cake. Measure the cake sides and the top of the cake using a length of string to ensure marzipan is rolled out to correct size.

2 Lifting marzipan over the centre of the cake using a pair of lifters.

3 Smoothing sides of marzipan using a pair of JEM Smoothers.

4 Smoothing the top and the sides of cake using the smoothers.

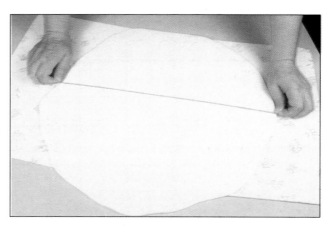

5 Measuring the cake board, the cake sides and the top of the cake before rolling out the sugarpaste.

6 Check the measurement of the rolled out sugarpaste before using the lifters to pick up the fondant.

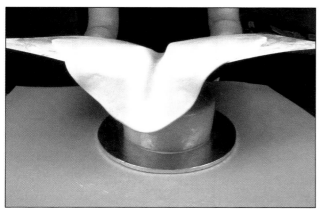

7 Carefully allow the fondant to fall on to centre of the marzipan cake using lifters.

8 Sufficient fondant to cover the cake and the cake board.

9 Trim the surplus fondant away. Smooth fondant against cake with hands, For a professional finish, use a pair of JEM smoothers.

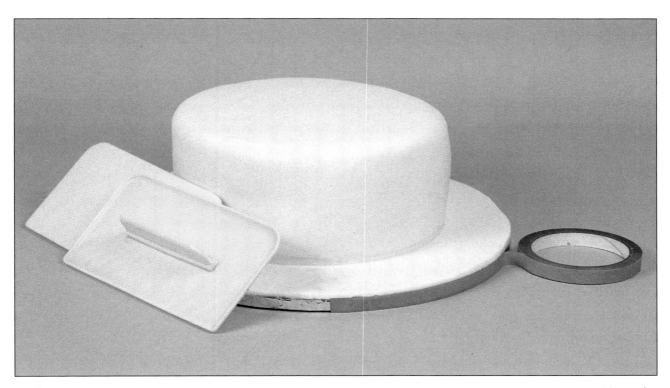

10 Place double sided tape around the edge of the cake board. Remove backing paper and attach ribbon of your choice to the side of the cake board.

CHRISTENING ROBES

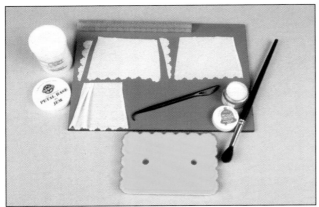

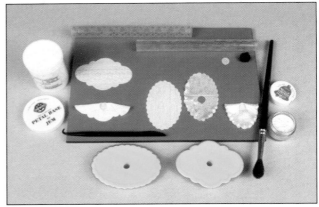

1 Lightly grease your work top surface with a little Petal Base. Roll out paste thinly using either the JEM Floral Drape or the Fabric Texture rollers for a different effect. The frilly card cutter (Set J4-1) is used to make the skirt. Use Tool 13A to trim the sides. The edge of the skirt may be frilled using Tool No. 15A. Apply a little lustre dust to the skirt. Pleat the skirt ensuring that the sides will be hidden behind the skirt.

2 Two alternative cutters are used for the bodice. Either the scalloped oval, Set J4-3, or the fancy oval type 1 Set J4-9. Use a small rose petal cutter to cut out the neck line. The edges may be frilled with Tool 15A if desired. Trim the robe with the miniature bow taken from the basket and bow cutter. Apply a little lustre dust. Attach the bodice to the skirt using a little petal glue.

THE CHRISTMAS TREE

An 11" (28cm) round cake was used for this project. The cake was placed on a 15" (38cm) round cake board. The cake was covered with royal blue sugarpaste.
The JEM Christmas Tree Set is used to decorate this cake.

1 Mix Squires Fern Green & Daffodil Yellow, creating a marble effect. Lightly grease the work top surface using JEM Petal Base. Roll out the paste thinly, ensuring that most of the yellow paste will be at the top of the tree. The edges of the tree are split using Tool No. 4B. In the same manner, work the cutouts in the tree beginning at the top of the tree and working downwards.

TRICK OF THE TRADE

A small piece of laminated board will assist you to do this.

Lift up cutouts. Place small pieces of sponge foam under cutouts and allow to dry.

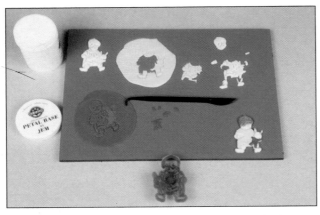

2 Cut out the child using flesh coloured paste. Roll out paste in the colour of your choice for the dress. Turn the cutter upside down, place the paste over the cutter, and using a ball tool, cut out the outline of the dress. Likewise cut out the hand and the bunny in a colour of your choice and build up the child. Or you may paint in the features using Squires Food Colouring.

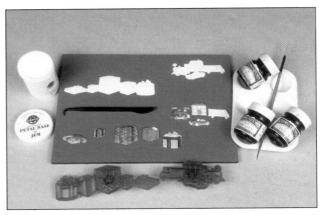

3 Cut out the toys, separate using JEM Tool No. 13A and paint using Squires Food Colouring of your choice. Cut out and separate the decorative gifts. Make enough gifts for under the tree and around the sides of the cake.

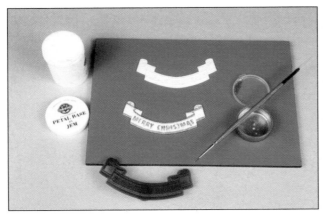

4 Cut out the Banner and paint the Merry Christmas and the outline in gold.

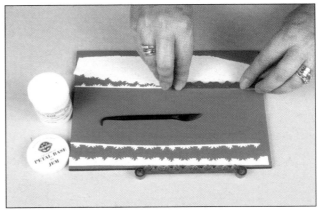

5 To create a frosty border, lightly grease a work top surface with Petal Base. Cut out a strip of Fairy Grass to place on the outside edge of the cake board.

DANCING TEDDIES CHRISTENING CAKE & DAFFODILS

An 8", (20 cm) round cake tin is used for this cake.   For display purposes the cake is placed on a 12" (30cm) cake board and then on a second cake board measuring 14" 35cm.   Cover the cake and the first board simultaneously in a soft yellow sugarpaste (rolled fondant).   The second board is covered separately.

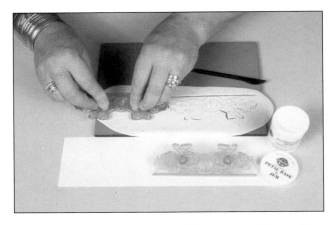

1 Using a light biscuit coloured flower paste roll out a long strip about 1 mm thick to cut out a continuous frieze using the Dancing Teddy cutter. The flower paste must be thick enough to absorb the embossed pattern in the cutter. The frieze should be long enough to fit around a 9" (23cm) or 10" (25cm) cake tin or dummy, to enable it to stand away from the cake sides.

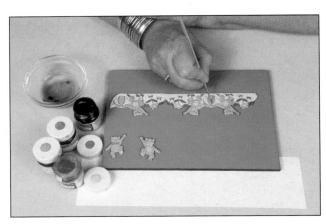

2 Paint in the features of the teddies using food colouring in the colours of your choice. Cut out individual teddies to place on the side of the cake. Place rolled out paste into the cutter over the teddy outline. Use a ball tool to press around the edges of the teddies causing them to be removed from the cutter.

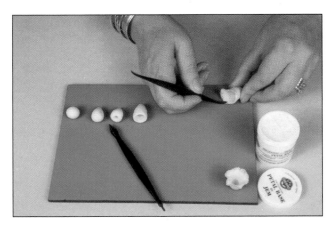

3 To prevent the frieze from sticking, lightly grease the larger cake tin, or cover a dummy with cling wrap. Place the frieze around the tin and leave to dry completely.

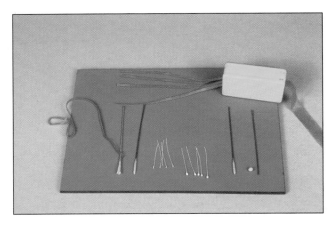

4 DAFFODIL
Six yellow stamens and a pistil are needed for the daffodil. Roll a tiny ball of yellow paste onto a 20 gauge taped wire to form the pistil. The top of the pistil should have three flat sides. Tape the stamens evenly around the pistil using 1/4 width shredded florist tape.

5 To make the trumpet, begin with a ball of yellow paste the size of a marble. Push Tool 2A into the centre of the ball to open it up. A little Petal Base on the work top surface will prevent the paste sticking to the board. Continue to turn the ball of paste as you thin the walls of the trumpet with tool No 2B. Use Tool 4A to lightly frill the edges at the top of the trumpet.

6 To make the back row of petals, form a small Mexican hat (point) with a wide brim. Hold the point over the centre of the cutter (Set B3) and press your fingers against the edge of the cutter causing the petals to be cut out. Place the pointed tip of the 'hat' into one of the holes in the JEM Mexican Petal Pad. Lightly soften the edges using ball tool No. 10B.

7 Cut out the second row of petals flat on a lightly greased work top surface. Vein the petals. Work the edges of the petals on a petal pad, and then place the inner row of petals into the back row of petals using a little petal glue to secure. Glue the trumpet into the centre of the petals.

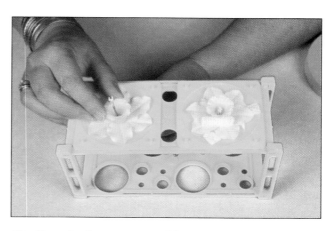

8 Place the flower into petal former No 5A and click this into position on a JEM Handy Holder. Using a little petal glue on the pistil, ease this through the centre of the trumpet. Leave to dry.

9 The foliage chosen to accompany the daffodils are chrysanthemum leaves found in Set L4A. Roll out green paste allowing for the insertion of a taped 26 gauge wire at the base of the leaf. Use Set V6 to vein the leaves. A ball tool is used to soften the edges of the foliage.

10 Dust the leaves with green and yellow petal dust and spray them with a cooking spray to give them a light sheen. To brighten the colour of the daffodil use Squires Daffodil petal dust.

11 The name is cut out using the JEM alphabet set. Lightly grease your work top surface and roll out the paste about 1mm thick. Cut out the lettering. This will give the lettering a dimension. If the paste is too thin, the lettering will appear flat and uninteresting. In the event of any letter sticking in a cutter, use a pin to remove it.

12 The side of the cake.

CAKE SIDES

Celebration showing the use of the S-Heart Scroll Cutter

Celebration cake showing the use of the Double Heart cutter.

CAKE SIDES

Celebration Cake showing the Hollow Oval cake side cutter.

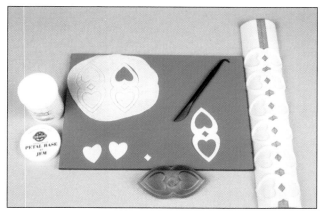

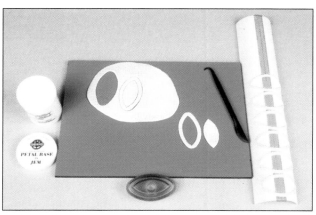

A half cylinder, or something similar, is required on which the side cutouts can dry. Mark a straight line down the centre of the cylinder/tube. This will assist in allowing all the cutouts to dry at the same angle.

ROMANTIC FRUITFUL DRAPES AND BOWS

Three square cakes measuring 7"(18cm), 9"(23cm) and 12"(30cm) are used for this cake. The cakes are covered in the usual way using cream sugarpaste. The cake boards are covered at the same time.

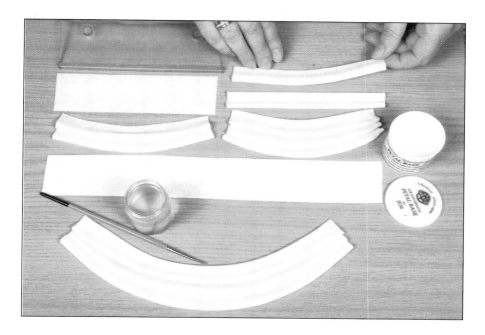

1 DRAPES AND BOWS
Lightly grease your work top surface with Petal Base or vegetable fat that is not too greasy. Using cream flower paste, roll out sufficient for each side of the cake. Use the endless JEM 5 strip cutter and cut out three lengths for each drape.
Fold two of the lengths in half. The third strip should be folded into the middle of itself forming a rounded edge on either side of the strip.
Using a little gum glue, place the strips one on top of the other ensuring that the double edged strip is on the top of the drape. Apply lustre dust. Attach to the side of the cake using a little gum glue.

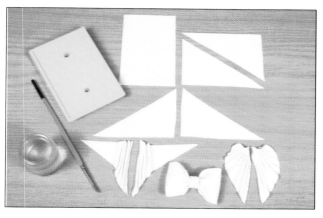

2 Using the same strip cutter, cut out a single length. Apply lustre dust. Fold sides into the centre of the strip. Lightly pinch together to form the bow. Cut a short piece about 5cm long and crease this strip to form the pleats in the "knot" of the bow.

3 To form the tails of the bow, Cutter J4-7 or 8 may be used. Cut out two separate pieces to form the tails and lightly apply lustre dust to each surface. Pleat each side evenly and shape as illustrated. Using a little gum glue, attach the bow to the tails and position on the cake.

4 VINE LEAVES AND GRAPES
Roll out green paste allowing for a ridge in the centre of each leaf for the insertion of taped 27 gauge wire. Cut out four sizes of leaves. Use a ball tool on a petal pad to soften the edges. Use a veiner to vein the leaves, or alternatively use the veining Tool No. 4B.

5 Place the leaves on bubble foam and allow them to dry. Dust the leaves with a selection of coloured dusts. Spray with a cooking spray to blend the colours. Mould the grapes using shaded flower paste. Insert 28 gauge wire into each grape. Twist 30 gauge wire, covered in quartered green tape, over a narrow paint brush to make the tendrils.

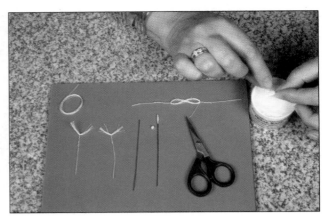

6 Tape the spray together using half width brown florist tape. Strengthen the spray by adding an extra 20 gauge taped wire. This will assist in holding the weight of the spray.

7 ORANGE & LEMON BLOSSOM
To make the centre of the blossom, roll white cotton around your fingers several times. Grip with very fine wire and cut the cotton in the middle. Place a little flower paste on a taped 26 gauge wire to form the pistil of the blossom. Use a little Petal Base on your fingers to strengthen the cotton stamens and give them a waxy appearance.

8 To make the blossom, begin with a little ball of flower paste. Shape it into a teardrop, using your fingers, flatten the edges. Use a small roller to form a Mexican Hat. Place this over the orange blossom cutter, Set No. B24. Press paste against the edges, cutting out the blossom.

9 Place the blossom on a Mexican petal pad with the back point of the blossom in one of the holes. Use a ball tool to soften and "cup" the petals. Place the cotton stamens into the centre of the flower.

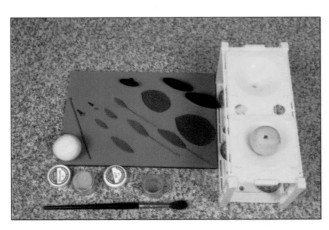

10 Using a mixture of almond paste and sugarpaste, mould small oranges. Use a grater to mark the outside of the orange. Cloves are placed into the base of the orange, and a taped hooked 18 gauge wire, is placed into the top of the orange. Allow the orange to dry in a petal former - No. 4B is suitable. When dry, dust with orange and a little green dust. Spray with a cooking spray to give the orange a light sheen. The orange leaves are made using three sizes of cutters taken from the water lily set, Set No. A8.

11 Tape the blossoms and buds together with the leaves and the oranges using green florist tape. To make a lemon, follow the directions to make the orange, but shape the lemon into a slightly oval shape and shade with yellow and green dust.

Murray and Emily Jane Pitt's Wedding Cake 10.02.2001
Detailed instructions to make the life-size roses can be found in "Simply Beautiful Cakes" by Jill Maytham.

The side of the cake.

DRAPE

Mix an equal amount of sugarpaste (rolled fondant) and flower paste together. On a lightly greased work top surface roll out a strip of paste approximately 6" (15 cm) wide and 12" (30cm) long for each drape. The size of the cake will determine the length of drape required. A plastic stencil mat (obtainable from Creative Cutters, Ontario, Canada) is placed over the paste.
Use a piece of sponge foam about the size of a bar of soap to brush lustre dust into the stencil. Remove stencil carefully. Create effect of material folds and drape over the cake. Secure with a little Tylose glue,

1   To make the stawberries see page 20.

2   The top tier.

3   The cake side.

Lemon Spray

Strawberry Fairies

A 12" (30 cm) square tin is used for this cake. A pattern is made about 5"(13 cm) deep to remove the corner of the cake. This is placed on top of the cake creating a tiered effect. The cake and the board are covered in a soft yellow sugarpaste in the usual way.

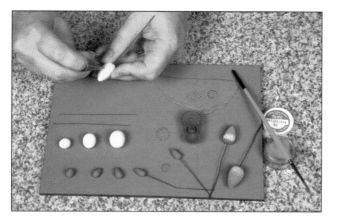

1 STRAWBERRIES
Mould several different sized strawberries by hand. A No. 1 icing nozzle is used to make the indentations on the strawberries. The very small strawberries are made in green flower paste, the others are made in a soft yellow paste. This allows the top of the strawberries to be dusted in shades of red to depict the different stages of ripening.
Different sized calyxes should be made for each strawberry and attached using a little gum glue.

2 Strawberry blossoms are made using two different sized blossom cutters. The stamens are made using yellow cotton centres that are twisted around a finger, gripped with fine fuse wire, and then cut and trimmed to fit into the blossoms.

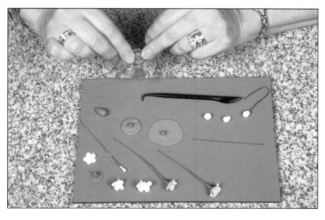

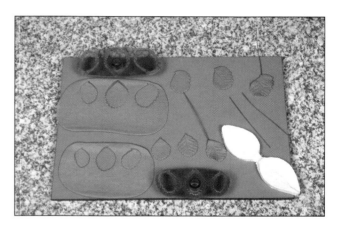

3 Green calyxes are made using the calyx cutters. Make a Mexican hat and place this over the cutter. Using your fingers press out the flower paste against the edge of the cutter causing the calyx to be cut out. Closed buds are made and petals marked using the No. 13A tool.

4 Make the leaves in two sizes, using the JEM strawberry leaf cutters (which are taken from a real plant). The cutters are designed to assist the decorator in the taping of the sprigs together correctly. Use a double-sided silicone leaf veiner to give the leaves character.

5 Tape the strawberries, blossom and leaves together using brown florist tape that has been shredded in half. Follow the pattern on the cutters for the correct taping of the leaves. The smaller leaves are shaded a brighter green than the larger leaves to create a more interesting effect.

6 Lightly grease your work top surface with a little Petal Base. Cut out the required number of fairy circle friezes. Trim the sides if individual pieces are required.

7 Roll out a small piece of flower paste and place this over the skirts of the fairies in the cutter. Using a ball tool work around the edges cutting out an extra skirt. A frilling tool with ridges (No. 15A) is applied to the edge of the skirt causing it to appear flared. Use a little gum glue to attach to the fairy.

8 Place the friezes on a piece of corrugated fibre glass, or something similar and allow to dry.

9 Using food colouring, paint fairies in appropriate colours. The toadstools may also be removed from the cutter in the same way as the extra skirt is cut out. See step 7 above.

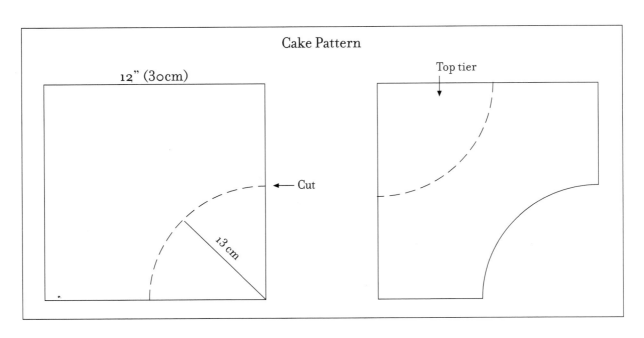

Cake Pattern

12" (30cm)

Top tier

← Cut

13 cm

21

GRAPEVINE FRIEZE

A comma cake tin is used for this cake, 10" (25cm) long and 7" (18cm) wide. The cake is placed on an oval board. The cake and the board were covered in the usual way.

The grape leaves are made using the Jem grape vine cutters They are made in shades of cream to light brown and then shaded with darker shades of brown . The leaves are then sprayed with a cooking spray and left to dry. The grapes are made in a darker brown. The spray is taped together using brown florist tape. A taped 20 gauge wire is added to the spray for additional strength.

1 Cut out an oval paper pattern smaller than the cake tin on which to set the inter-locking grapevine pieces. See step 4.

Lightly grease your work top surface with a little Petal Base and, using light brown flower paste, cut out sufficient pieces of the grapevine cutwork embroidery cutter to fit around the top of the cake, forming an oval.

2 Mix sufficient royal icing to a soft peak consistency for the brush embroidery. To this a little piping gel may be added to prevent the icing from drying out too fast. Using a No. 1 icing nozzle, pipe a small section of the outline on the grapevine pattern. Use a damp paint brush to pull the edges into the pattern.

The grapes are built up separately by applying a little pressure to the tube to form each grape. Begin working on the grapes that would be in the background, finishing with the grapes that would be on top of the bunch.

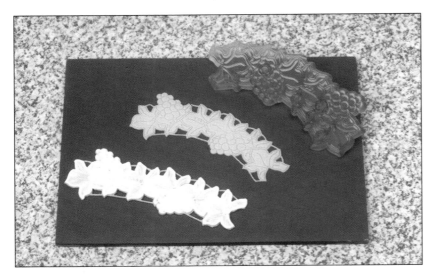

TRICK OF THE TRADE

A damp paintbrush should be used to pull the edges into the pattern.

Complete a whole section before stopping for a break.

3 A finished grapevine frieze.

4 Using a No. 4 strip cutter, cut out a long strip of flower paste to fit onto the oval pattern that fits on to the cake. To give this frame extra strength, additional Tylose is worked into the flower paste.

Using royal icing, secure the inter-locking grapevine pieces to the oval frame and allow to dry completely.

Attach to the cake using royal icing to secure.

5 Use dark brown paste to cut out a strip using Strip No. 3, long enough to fit around the cake. Twist and attach to the base of the cake.

Use the same colour paste to cut out a message.

THE TEDDY BEAR'S PICNIC

A 12" (30 cm) tear drop cake tin is used for this cake. This is placed on a 16" (40 cm) oval cake board. Both the cake and the board are covered in light green sugarpaste. Gooseberry green is used to colour the sugarpaste.
Note: Instructions to make the jasmine can be found on page 45.

1 Cut out the cobblestone wall in light grey flower paste. Sufficient length to close the gap from one side of the cake to the other to form an oval shape is required. Apply a mixture of petal dusts to create an aged effect, finish with Squires Eidelweiss

2 Place the length of the cobblestone wall on a lightly greased oval cake tin to dry. Position on the cake board with a little royal icing to secure.

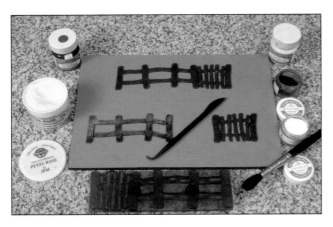

3 Cut out the rustic fence and gate using the special cutter. Roll the paste (not too thin) on a lightly greased work surface. Tool 13 is used to separate the gate from the fence. This is dried flat and joined to the cobblestone wall with a little gum glue. The fence is lightly painted with Eidelweiss colouring.

4 Cut out the fence and place on the greased tin to dry. Shade the fence with light petal dust. Attach to cake top with a little royal icing.

5 Cut out the bears using the Dress-a-Teddy Cutter. Shade the flower paste with Teddy Bear Brown. Whilst the paste is soft, texture it with a clean toothbrush. To give the teddies a 3D effect, place small bits of flower paste to pad the tummy, arms and legs and also the snout. Seal the back and front of each teddy.

6 Teddy bears in different positions may be made using the same principle. Use Tool 13 to remove head, arms and legs as desired to create different poses. Cut out the dungarees in blue and attach to the teddy before placing the feet in the sitting position.

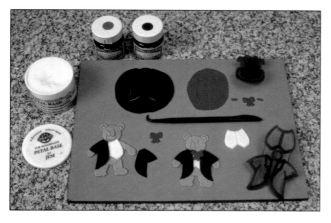

7 Cut out the waistcoat in white and the jacket in black flower paste for the daddy teddy. The red bow is cut out using the apron bow.

8 Make a light blue dress for the girl teddy. Tool 15A frills the end on the dress and the skirt. Trim this with the little bow. The mummy teddy is wearing a skirt, blouse and an apron. The baby teddy is textured with a clean tooth brush and trimmed with the little bow. The basket is filled with cutouts using the smallest Daisy Centre Stamp.

9 The Woodland Tree Stump cutter is used for the tree stump. Cut out double and allow to dry before placing on top of the cake. The tree stumps against the cake are cut out singly. The stumps are then shaded with lighter petal dusts.

10 A length of fairy grass is cut out and used to trim the wall, fence and woodland tree stump.

11 Use the Fairy Feast cutter to cut out the food. Separate the items using Tool 13A. Liquid food colouring may be used to paint the different items.

12 When the food is painted and the woodland tree stump is dry, use a little gum glue to attach the food to the top of the tree stump. Allow to dry before placing the tree stump on the cake with royal icing.

RECIPES

TYLOSE FLOWER PASTE

INGREDIENTS:

egg white	35ml	31g	1
sifted icing sugar	250ml	140g	1 cup
Tylose C1000p	20ml	11g	2 rounded tsp

METHOD:

Lightly beat an egg white. Add sifted icing sugar slowly until a soft peak consistency is reached. Add the Tylose C1000p. The mixture will immediately thicken. Gradually add more sifted icing sugar until a pliable texture is achieved. Rub a little white Petal Base or white vegetable fat on your hands and work paste thoroughly. Paste should not be sticky nor should it be too hard.

Store in a sealed plastic bag in a sealed plastic container. Paste is ready to use immediately.

Note:
- If you have used as extra large egg white you may need to increase the amount of Tylose slightly.
- If the paste is too soft, you may need to work in extra sifted icing sugar.
- If the paste is too stiff, work in extra egg white.

TRICK OF THE TRADE

A variation of this recipe is to add sugarpaste (rolled fondant) to the flower paste.

TYLOSE GLUE, PETAL GLUE, GUM GLUE

Mix 5ml Tylose C1000p in 200ml water.
Allow the tylose to dissolve.
5ml icing sugar may be added to this.

TRICK OF THE TRADE

Additional Tylose will strengthen the glue.

CARD PASTILLAGE RECIPE

5ml Gelatine
30ml Water
250ml Icing Sugar
15ml Tylose C1000p
5ml Cream of Tartar

Dissolve the gelatine in the cold water over a bowl of hot water.

Sift dry ingredients. Make a well in the centre, add the gelatine and knead.

Should you require a stiffer paste, additional icing sugar may be added. Roll out on JEM Petal Base.

All the flowers in this book have been made using the Tylose recipe.

WILD ROSE WEDDING CAKE

A 5" (12,5 cm) and a 8" (20 cm) square cake are needed for this wedding cake. The cake boards are 7" (17,5 cm), 12"(30 cm). Both the cakes and the cake boards are covered simultaneously in pink sugarpaste (rolled fondant). The base board measures 14" (35 cm) and is covered separately.

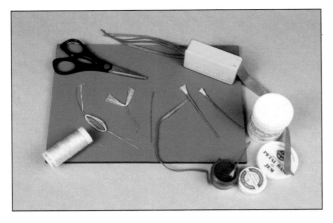

1 WILD ROSES
The centres for the roses are made by twisting cotton several times around your finger. Grip the cotton in the middle using soft wire. Cut the cotton in the middle. Tape the cotton on to a 26 gauge wire. Dip the tips of the cotton into a little Petal Base and then into a little brown pollen.

2 Use the 60 mm Easy Rose cutter. Roll out the paste on a lightly greased work top surface. Cut out the flower. Place the flower on a petal bad. Use Tool 10B to soften the petals.

3 Make smaller and larger wild roses by using the 50 mm and 80 mm cutters. The calyx is found in Set A10. Curl the petals inwards and backwards using a cocktail stick. Dust the centre of the wild roses yellow and the petals pink. Make a little ball of green paste to represent the 'hip' for the calyx.

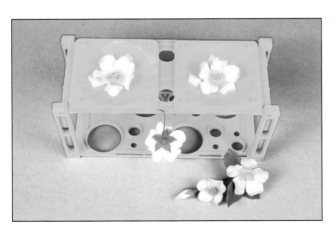

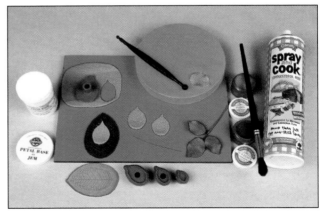

4 Place the flowers in Petal formers 5A and click these into the Handy Holder and leave to dry.
Note the calyx in the picture.

5 The foliage is made using the Small Rose Leaves Set L10. Roll out the paste in green allowing for the insertion of 26 gauge taped wire. Cut out sufficient leaves for the number of sprigs required. Remember the largest leaf is at the end of the sprig.

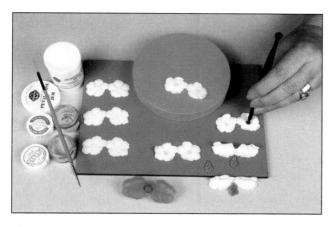

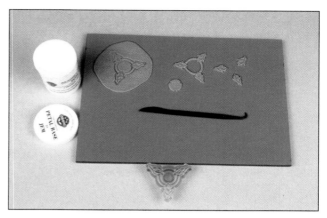

6 The side border is made using the small Briar Rose Cutwork Embroidery Cutter

Cut out sufficient flowers to place around the edge of the first cake board. Lightly frill the edges on a petal pad and use ball tool 10A to indent the centre of the flower.
Lightly dust the centres yellow and the petals pink.

7 Cut out the leaf circle found in the same set. Separate the leaves and place these next to the cutwork pattern on the side of the cake board.

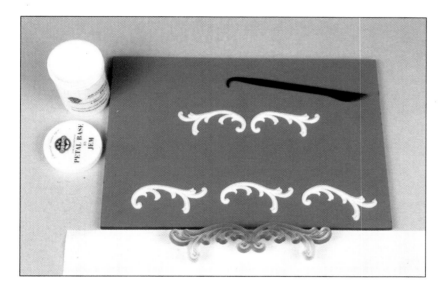

8 Use the double scroll cutter and cut out as many pieces as required for the side of the cake. Only one side has been used to create the effect in the picture.

9 The side of the cake.

GEOMETRICAL DESIGNS FOR ANY OCCASION

An effective and simple idea suitable for any celebration.

A 6" (15 cm) square cake and a 10" (25 cm) cake board is used for this design.
Cover the cake and the board simultaneously in white sugarpaste (rolled fondant).

1 Flower paste in three different shades of blue is used to create the design. Roll out the paste on a work top surface lightly greased with Petal Base. Cut out sufficient pieces to form the pattern. It is advisable to create the pattern off the cake. Begin in the middle of the cake and assemble the design. Strip No. 2 is used for the border around the base of the cake. A simple pattern is created for the cake board.

A Medley Of Christmas Cards

CARD PASTILLAGE RECIPE

5ml Gelatine
30ml Water
250ml Icing Sugar
15ml Tylose C1000p
5ml Cream of Tartar

Dissolve the gelatine in the cold water over a bowl of hot water.
Sift dry ingredients.
Make a well in the centre, add the gelatine and knead. Should you require a stiffer paste, additional icing sugar may be added. Roll out on JEM Petal Base.

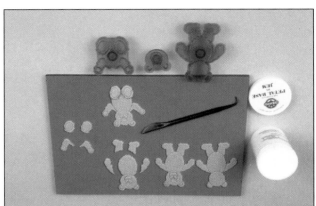

1 To create teddy bears in different positions, you may cut out additional legs and arms using the cutter provided for this purpose. Teen Tool 13A is a useful tool to remove the legs and arms. Use Tylose Glue to attach the new arms and legs to the teddy's body.

2 Likewise, if you wish the teddy to look to the left or the right, remove the head and use one of the profile cutters in the set. Paint in the facial features and claws using black food colouring.

TEDDY CHRISTMAS CARD

3 If you wish the teddy to be looking forward use the face embosser. Texture the teddy using a new toothbrush. To create different facial features on your teddy bears you will need to make a tiny nose. The smallest JEM Daisy Centre Stamp is ideal for this purpose. The head without the facial features represents the back of the teddy's head.

4 Cut out the clothes of your choice and place them on the teddies using a little gum glue to secure.

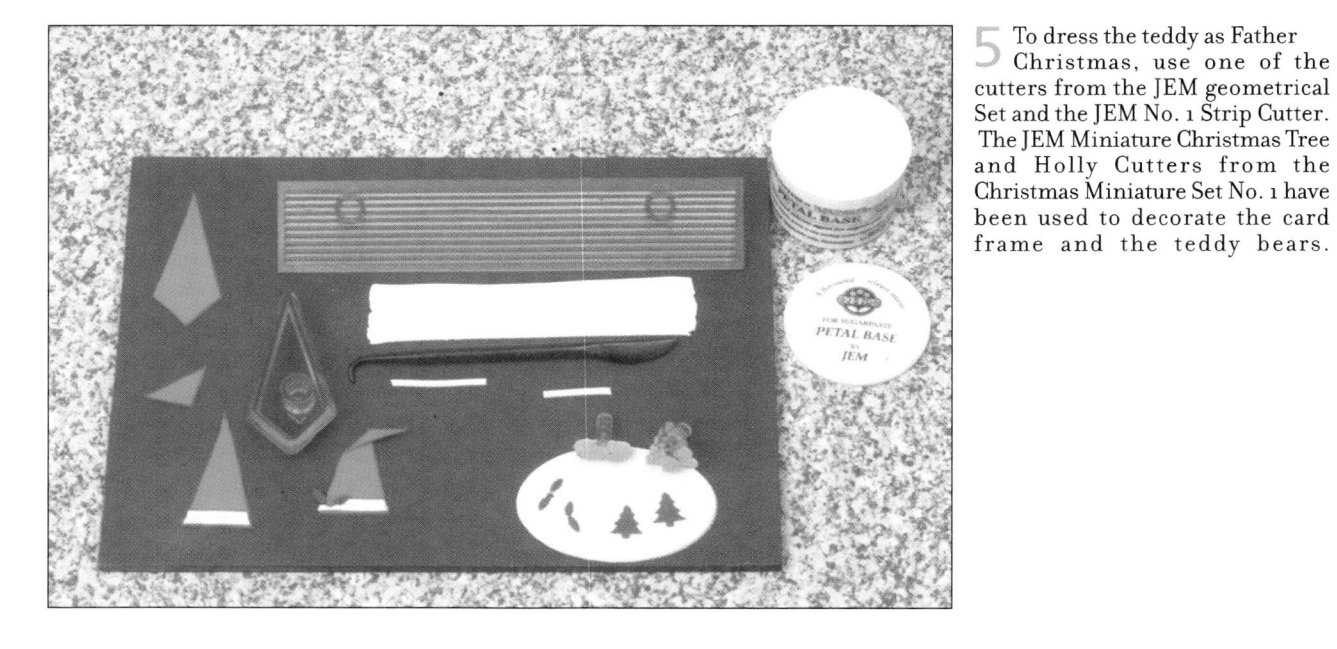

5 To dress the teddy as Father Christmas, use one of the cutters from the JEM geometrical Set and the JEM No. 1 Strip Cutter. The JEM Miniature Christmas Tree and Holly Cutters from the Christmas Miniature Set No. 1 have been used to decorate the card frame and the teddy bears.

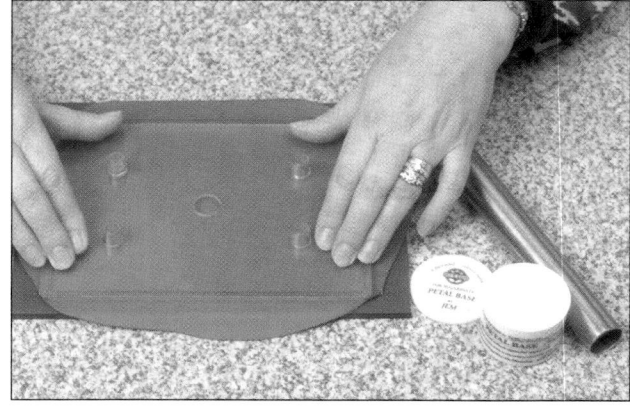

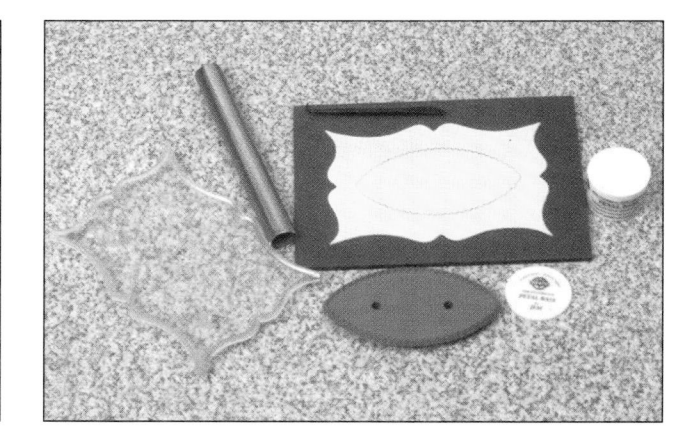

6 Lightly grease a small board with Jem Petal Base. Roll out sufficient paste using the Card Pastillage recipe. The card needs to be thin and should not be moved off the board until it is almost dry. This card requires a back and a front. The cutter used is the JEM Large Greeting Card.

7 Using soft lemon coloured paste, create a frame for the scene using the JEM Plaque cutter Set P1. Cut out the middle of the frame using Set J5-16. Allow to "air" dry until the frame forms a skin. Place in position on the card front.

CHRISTMAS WREATH CARD

1 Using the same card pastillage recipe, cut out the circle using the medium JEM Disc Cutter 86mm. The smallest disc cutter, 71mm is used to create the wreath. A little Tylose Glue was used to attach it to the circle.

SANTA REINDEER SILHOUETTE CARD

The colour of the front of this card was mixed from blue and black. The back of the card represents moonlight yellow. The card was cut out in the same way as indicated above.
The JEM Medium Disc Cutter 86mm was used to represent the moon. The Star is taken from the JEM Christmas Miniature Set No. 1 and cut into the card front whilst it is still wet.

The sleigh and the teddy are found in the JEM Christmas Miniature Set No. 2. To make Father Christmas fit into the sleigh, remove the teddy's legs and his right ear. This will create the impression that he is guiding his reindeer. The reindeer are from the JEM Christmas Miniature Set No. 1.
The bow is made using the JEM Bow Cutter size 2.

2 The holly and poinsettias are cut out from the JEM Christmas Garland Frieze cutter. Use a little Petal Base and roll out white paste thinly. Pick up the paste and place the greasy side on to the face of the cutter. Use JEM Tool No.6 and press against the cutting edge of the holly and poinsettia to cut them out of the frieze.

3 Use food colouring to paint the petals and leaves avoiding the veins. The bow is made using the JEM Strip No. 3 cutter.

POINSETTIA CHRISTMAS CARD

This card was cut out in the same way. The front of the of the card is white and the back of the card yellow.
The JEM 86mm Disc Cutter is used for the front of the card.
JEM Strip No. 3 is used to create the frame and the bow.
Use Tylose glue to attach the strip to the edge of the card.
The poinsettia is made using the JEM L5 set.

Detailed instructions for this flower can be found in "Sugar Flowers" or "Simply Beautiful Cakes" by Jill Maytham.

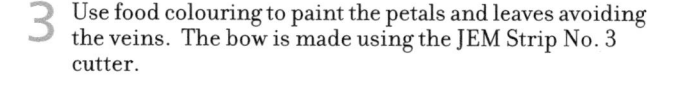

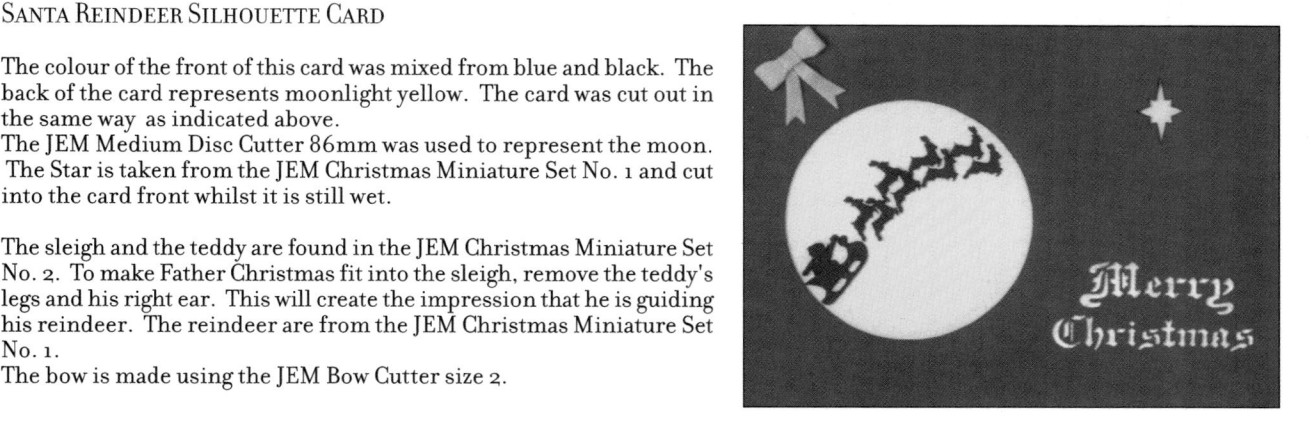

VICTORIAN SCROLL AND POINSETTIA CARD

Roll out card - back and front and described above. Using JEM J5-5 cut out the centre of the front of the card and allow to dry. Using the JEM Christmas Garland Frieze and red and green paste, cut out the individual pieces as described in step 2 above.
Place these in position on the card using Tylose Glue to secure.
Use a little food colouring to paint in berries and centres of the poinsettia.
To make the scrolls and the bow, the JEM Double Scroll Cutter is used together with the JEM No. 1 Bow Cutter and red flower paste. Hi-lite with gold dust mixed with a drop of alcohol.
Use red royal icing and a stencil for the message.

IDEAS FOR CAKE TOPS

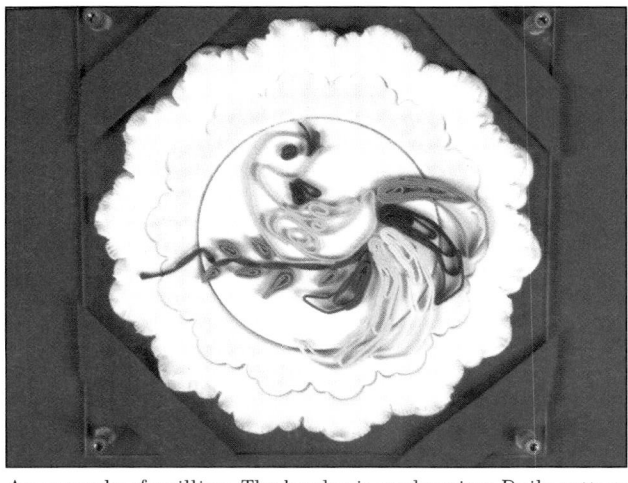

An example of quilling. The border is made using Doily cutters 160mm and 125mm. The centre is cut out using Disc No.71, Strip Cutter No. 1 is used together with Quilling Tool No 11 to create the picture. Detailed instructions can be found in the book *"Simply Beautiful Cakes" by Jill Maytham*.

Create a Bird House using a champagne glass found in Set J6-17 together with Strip No. 5 embossed with Strip No. 4 to create a wood effect. The sword fern cutter L2B represents a branch of a tree. The blue birds are found in Set J6-9 and the geranium leaf in Set L4C, is used for the bush.

An elegant fan. Set J5-16 contains a double fan blade cutter. Decorate the fan using Embossing tool Set 1 while the paste is still soft. While the paste is still wet remember to cut a small hole using a No. 1 icing nozzle at the base of each blade. This is for the insertion of soft wire to grip the fan blades together.

A striking design suitable for the top of a cake. Strip No.1 and Strip No. 2 are used together with the Fantasy Cutwork Cutter.

Dramatic Sunflowers. The shaped card front was made using the outline of the Bridal Rose Frieze cutter. Make the sunflowers using the large strawberry calyx cutter. The centres are made using the daisy centre stamps. A stencil is used for the message.

Just Married. The Dress a Teddy set is used to create this picture. Make the bed frame using Strip No. 1. The top of the bed is made using the border from the Oval frieze cutter. The floral drape roller is used for the curtains and Bow No. 1 for the tie backs. The JEM alphabet set is used for the message. The hearts can be found in the miniature wedding set.

Children's Party Places Names. Make the children feel special by creating individual name cards. Set J5-1 and J5-2 are used in the illustration. The special triangle cutter found in Set J4-11 is used to make the place names stand up. The love birds are found in Set J6-9, the Dress a Teddy set, the kitten set and wild ducks are some examples of what may be used. The JEM alphabet is used for the names.

The fantasy fish have been made using the hibiscus cutter found in Set B14. The fish tail is the petal skirt found in the Little Darlings set. The other small fish are made using frangipani cutters found in Sets A7 and B34. The seaweed is made using the silver grey leaf Set L6B and Set L6C. The fish eyes and the bubbles are made using the daisy centre stamps. The background is made using Cutter Set P1.

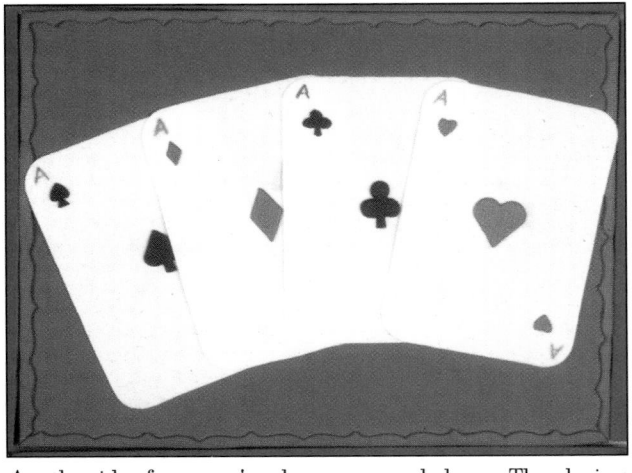

Another idea for a man's cake, or any card player. The playing card is found in Set J5-5 the card suites are found in Set A-20. The border is taken from the oval frieze cutter. The smaller hearts are found in the wedding miniatures, Set 2. The small diamond is cut freehand. The small club is made using the miniature bouvardia cutter, with one petal removed, Set B15. The spade is made using a small heart and the tail is made freehand.

A winning idea for a cake top. Three sizes of doily cutter have been frilled using Tool 15A to frill the edges. The centre is the 71mm doily disc. The tails of the rosette are made using Strip No. 4 and the JEM alphabet and Numeral cutters are used for the 1st.

A different idea for a greeting card using the playing card J5-5 to remove the inside of the card. The leaf scroll forms the pattern and a stencil is used for the 40.

An idea for a cake top suitable for a man. The interlocking Grapevine frieze cutter is painted and a bunch of grapes is place in the centre.

37

A cake top suggestion. The Fantasy Cutter is used showing the flower removed from the cutter.

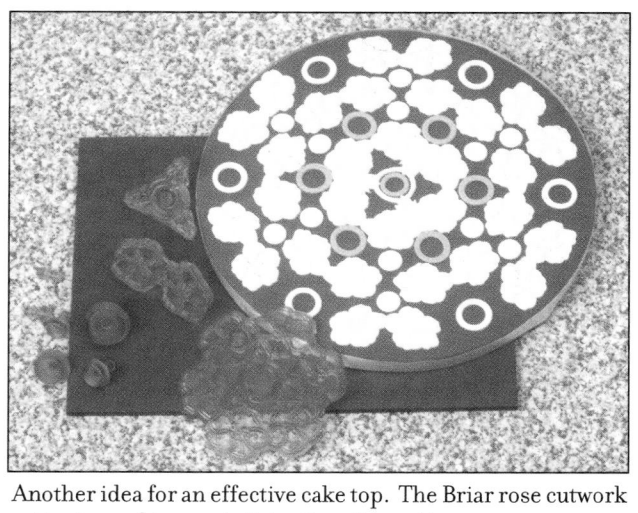

Another idea for an effective cake top. The Briar rose cutwork cutter is used to create this attractive pattern.

101 Dalmations is always a popular idea with children. The dogs are found in Set J6-8. The scalloped Circle is Set P3. The centre is cut out using Disc 120mm. The trimming around the border is the double scroll cutter. The numerals are found in Set A1.

The soccer ball. The background is made using the scalloped circle Set P3. The ball is made from the hexagonal cutter found in the geometrical cutters. When you have sufficient pieces for the ball, use the large disc 120mm to trim the edges of the ball. Use the JEM alphabet for the message.

Fun with JEM - The large scroll is created using the large greeting card. The outside edges of this card are trimmed using the outside edges of the scroll cutter J4-12. The edges are then curled inwards and the card is aged using a selection of soft petal dusts and then trimmed with gold. The miniature roses are made using the tiny petal cutter found in Set B15. The rose leaves are also found in this set - simply remove one of the miniature bouvardia's petals. Use very fine wire if you wish to create a spray. The calyx for the miniature roses is the five petal daisy wheel cutter.

The cutwork daisy scroll cutter is used for the centre of this card. The centre is cut out using the doily 125 mm cutter. The No. 2 strip is used for the border and the double scroll is embossed into the sides of the card.

A greeting card idea using the grapevine cutter. Use the oval card J5-16 to remove the centre. A stencil is used for the message.

Another idea using the grapevine cutter and the double scroll cutter.

The rectangular scroll cutter P1 is used for the white background of the card. The centre is made using cutter J5-16. The Bridal Rose Frieze cutter is used to decorate the greeting card.

Another idea using the Bridal Rose Frieze cutter. The centre is made using the rectangular scroll cutter J4-13.

The small double cutter found in the Briar Rose Cut work set is used to decorate this card. The centre is cut out using the rectangular scroll cutter J4-13. The double scroll cutter is used for the added decoration. A stencil is used for the message.

The pansy cutwork embroidery cutter is painted in different shades and used to make this greeting card. A stencil is used for the 18.

Dress-a-Teddy steps. Use the face embosser for the teddy to look straight ahead. Remove the head and change to either a left or right profile. Remove legs to make a sitting teddy, and remove arm/s for different positions. Texture with a toothbrush and paint in features using black food colouring and a fine paintbrush. The blank teddy is it's back.

The Dress-a-Teddy set is used to create this picture together with the optional extras. Disc No 86 is used to remove the centre.

The wedding. The Dress-a-Teddy set is used for this card. The little flowers are made from the five petal daisy wheel. The double scroll is embossed. A little tulle is used for the veil. A stencil is used for the message.

The Happy Birthday banner is made from Strip No. 4. The JEM alphabet cutters are used for the message. The teddies are from the Dress-a-Teddy set. The streamers are made using strip No. 1. Twist them around a thin paintbrush or a cocktail stick. The balloons are made using the inside of a "O" alphabet cutter. The border is made using the window frieze cutter.

The valentine teddies are made using the Dress-a-Teddy set. The basket and bow cutter is also used together with the miniature hearts found in the wedding set. The small oval cutters found in Set J4-4 is used for the frames. The double scroll is used for the background.

Another valentine card using the Dress-a-Teddy set, the Bridal Rose Frieze, the double scroll and the miniature hearts found in the wedding set, and the heart found in the card suites, Set A20.

A simple design for a card or cake top. Large doily cutter 160mm for the background. 120mm disc for the centre. The leaf scroll cutter and the double scroll cutter.

Cake side design. A leaf scroll and the double scroll and part of the Elegant scroll is used for this cake side.

Cake side design. Remove the flower found in the fantasy cutwork flower to create this design. The double scroll is also used.

Another cake side design using the Cutwork daisy embroidery cutter and Strip No.1

Using the Large Card Cutter cut out a back and front card in contrasting colours. Use the Fantasy Cutwork Cutter and emboss the pattern onto the top card. Remove the cut out pieces with a sharp knife. Cut out individual flowers and leaves from the same cutter to form a pattern on the front of the card. The cross cutter found in Set J6-14 completes the picture.

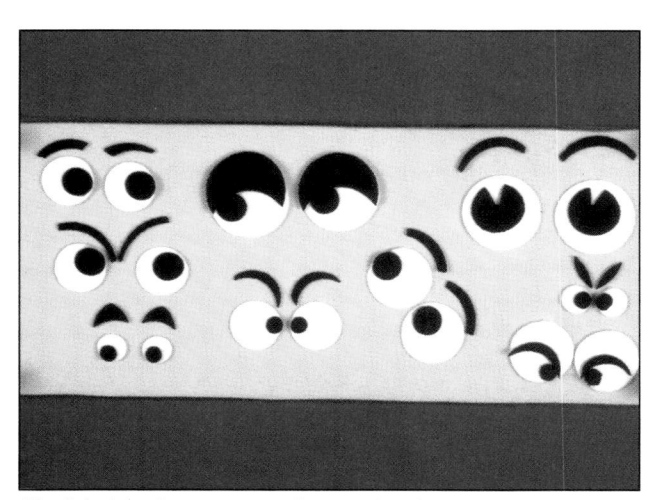

Useful ideas for eyes to make novelty characters using the daisly centre stamps in different ways.

The Christmas tree set is used to create this scene. The decorative gift cutter is used and the gifts separated. The tree is decorated with daisy centre stamps and the little bow from the basket and bow set.

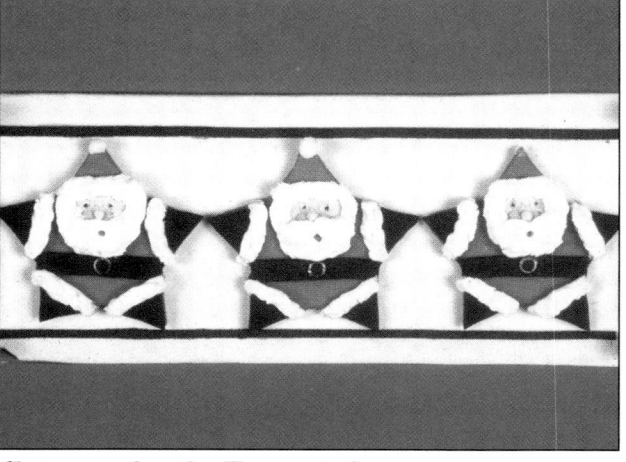

Christmas cake side. The novelty Santa is made using the star found in JEM 4-14. Santa's belt is made using Strip No. 2. Strip No. 1 is the border. The triangles are found in the geometrical set.

Unwrapping gifts. Cut out the child and bunny in flesh coloured paste. Using different colours cut out the individual parts of the body and dress, building up the picture. Alternatively, the child could be painted using food colouring. Strip No. 1 is used for the garland. The oval is cutter J5-16. The food is taken from the fairy feast cutter and has been separated.

Cut away the bottom half of the Christmas tree to the size required. Use daisy centre stamps to decorate the tree. The decorative gift cutter is used and the gifts separated. The No. 1 strip cutter is used for the streamers. Twist the paste around a thin paint brush or a cocktail stick. The frame is doily cutter No. 160mm and the middle is cut out using disc 120mm.

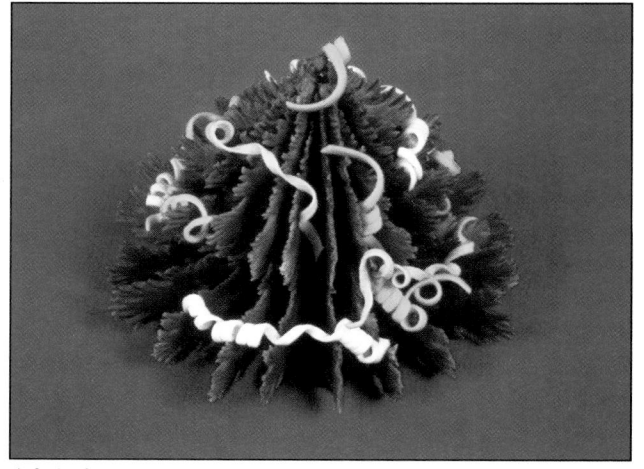

A 3-D Christmas tree for the top of a cake. Cut out about nine trees to the height/size required then cut each section of the tree in half. Lightly frill the outside edges of the tree. Allow the branches to dry completely. Use the 71mm disc to form a small cone on which to stick the dry branches. Allow to dry completely. Green Royal icing is needed for this exercise. Trim the tree using Strip No. 1 for streamers.

PRAM CHRISTENING CAKE & JASMINE

An 8" (20cm) round cake tin is used for this cake.
The cake and the 12" (30cm) cake board are covered simultaneously in blue sugarpaste (rolled fondant).

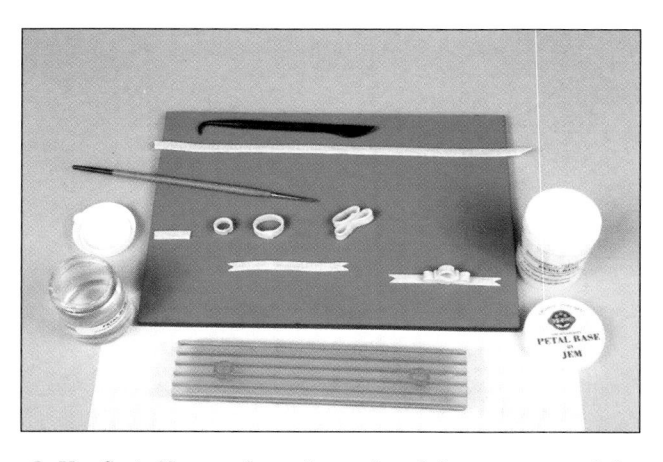

1 Use Strip No. 2 to form the top band that goes around the cake. Roll out the paste very thinly to make the side bow. Cut out a strip to form the tails of the bow and then form three loops to fit one into the other. Use a little petal glue to secure and attach to the side of the cake.

2 To make the band to support the prams roll out flower paste long enough to fit around a 10" (25cm) cake tin that has been lightly greased, or a dummy which is covered with cling film.

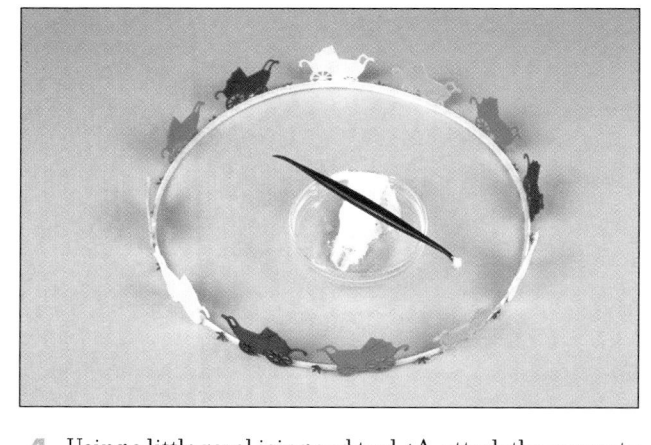

3 On a lightly greased board, roll out flower paste about 1 mm thick in shades of blue and white and cut out the prams. Allow to air dry for several minutes before removing the pieces between the spokes. Leave to dry completely.

4 Using a little royal icing and tool 4A, attach the prams to the circular band ensuring they are evenly spaced and are standing upright.

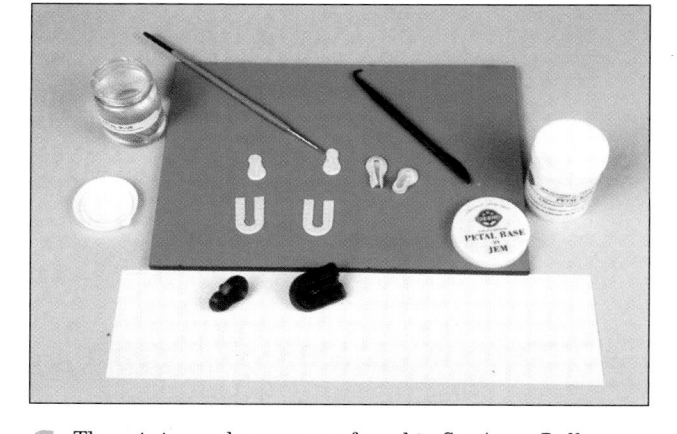

5 Cut out the message using the JEM alphabet set. Different shades of blue and white have been used. Roll out the flower paste about 1 mm thick on a lightly greased work top surface and cut out the lettering. If a letter should stick in the cutter, simply use a pin to remove it.

6 The miniature bootees are found in Set A19. Roll out paste about 1mm thick to cut out the sole. Roll out the paste thinly for the top of the bootees. Use a paint brush to apply a little petal glue around the sole of the bootee and attach the top of the bootee to this. The wider part of the sole represents the toe and the narrow part the heel. A narrow strap may be made freehand, or you may use Strip No. 1. Pipe a button on the bootees, remembering to make a left and a right shoe.

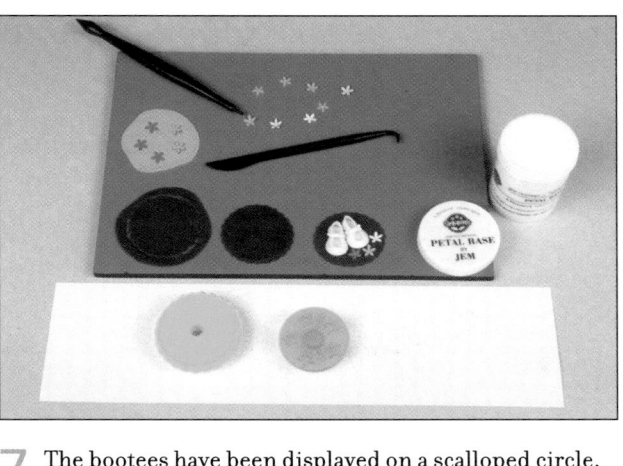

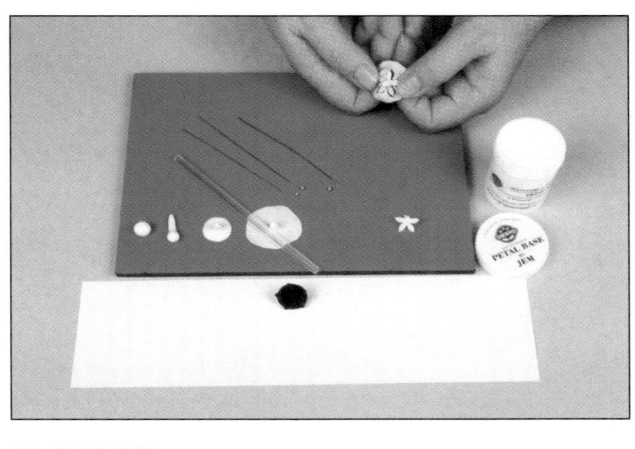

7 The bootees have been displayed on a scalloped circle, plaque J4-5. The baby flowers are made using the five petal daisy wheel cutter. Cut out baby flowers in different shades and place around the edge of the cake board.

8 JASMINE
To make the jasmine roll a small ball of paste about the size of a pea. Form this into a pear shape. Flatten the base and create a Mexican hat effect.
Use the jasmine cutter found in Set B16. Place the point of the Mexican hat in the middle of the cutter and press your fingers around the edge of the cutter causing the petals to be cut out.

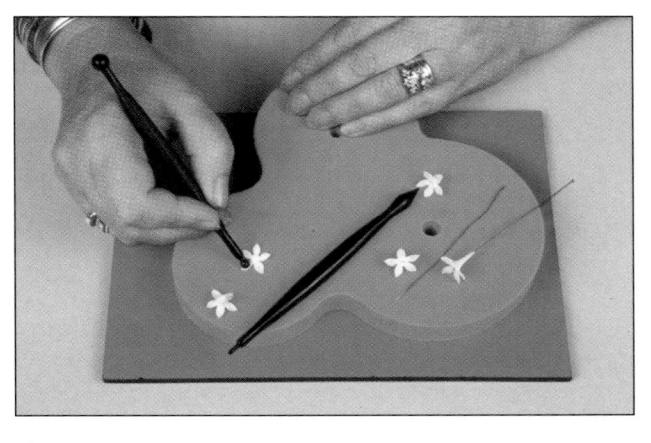

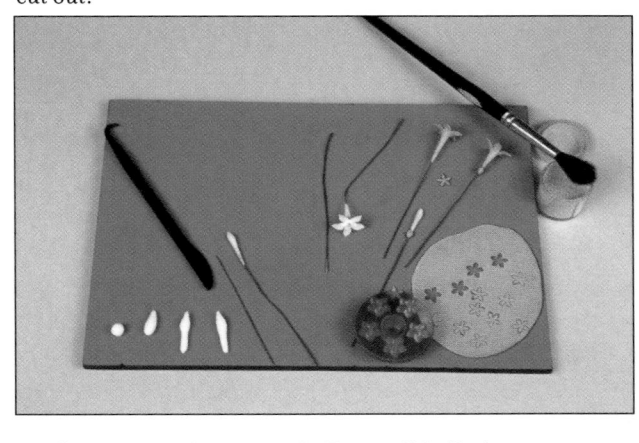

9 Place the pointed 'hat' part of the flower into a Mexican Petal Pad and use tool 10A to flatten the individual petals. Use tool No 2B to make a point in the centre of the flower.

10 To make the buds. Roll a small ball, shape into a teardrop - use Tool no. 13A to form the petals on the buds. The five petal daisy wheel cutter is used for the calyx on the flowers and buds. These are cut out in green paste. The buds and the back of the flowers are dusted in a maroon shade.

11 The foliage is found in Set A14. The pointed leaves are rolled out to allow for the insertion of taped wire, gauge 26, into the base of each leaf. The leaves are assembled with the large leaf at the end of the sprig. Dust the leaves in a dark green petal dust and spray with a cooking spray to give them a light sheen. When they are dry, tape the leaves and the flowers together with florist tape.

12 The side of the cake.

FANTASY CUTWORK CAKE & FRANGIPANI

An 8 " (20 cm) square cake is used for this cake.
The first cake board is 12"(30 cm) and the second cake board is 15" (37,5 cm).   The cake and the first cake board are covered simultaneously in white sugarpaste (rolled fondant).   The second cake board is covered separately.

1 Use a rich cream flower paste to cut out the Fantasy Cutwork design for this cake. Four pieces are cut out for the top of the cake and left to dry. Eight pieces are cut out for the base of the cake and the bottom cake board. The double square side cutter is used to make the pattern fit into the corners of the cake and cake board. The flower in the pattern is painted a soft yellow with a touch of orange for a deeper centre.

2 The pattern is enhanced by using the double scroll cutter on the top and sides of the cake.

3 FRANGIPANI
The frangipani cutter, Set A7 is used for the flowers. Roll out the paste thinly. Cut five petals. Curl the left side of each petal using a ball tool on a piece of soft sponge. Allow the petals to dry slightly until they are holding their shape.

Place the petals one into the other creating a fan. Use a little petal glue at the base of each petal to hold them together. Keep the tops of the petals almost level. Hold the petals upside down. Twist the base.

Insert a taped 26 gauge wire with a small tip of flower paste on the end of it and ease this through the centre of the flower.

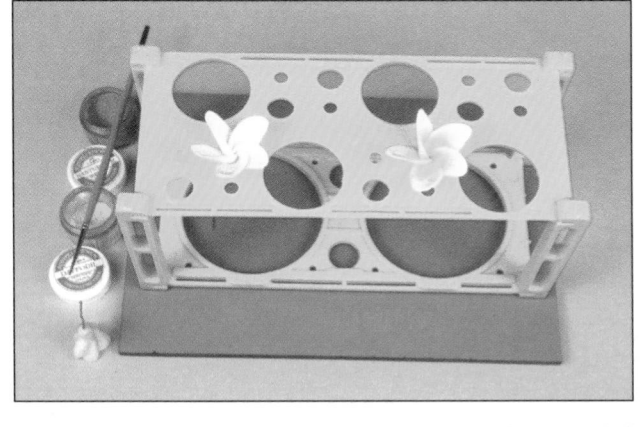

4 Allow the flowers to dry supported in the holes provided for this purpose in the Handy Holder. Gently ease open the petals. Dust the centre of the flowers with yellow petal dust and a touch of orange to create the depth of colour.

5 The waterlily cutters found in Set A8 are used for the foliage. Roll out green paste allowing for the insertion of a 26 gauge taped wire. Vein the leaves using the rose leaf veiner Set V1. Dust the leaves in a dark petal dust. Spray with a cooking spray to give the leaves a light sheen. Make the buds by rolling a piece of white flower paste into a cone. Use Tool 13A to make petal marks on the cone. Twist the cone to create the correct effect. Insert a taped 26 gauge wire into the bud for the stem.

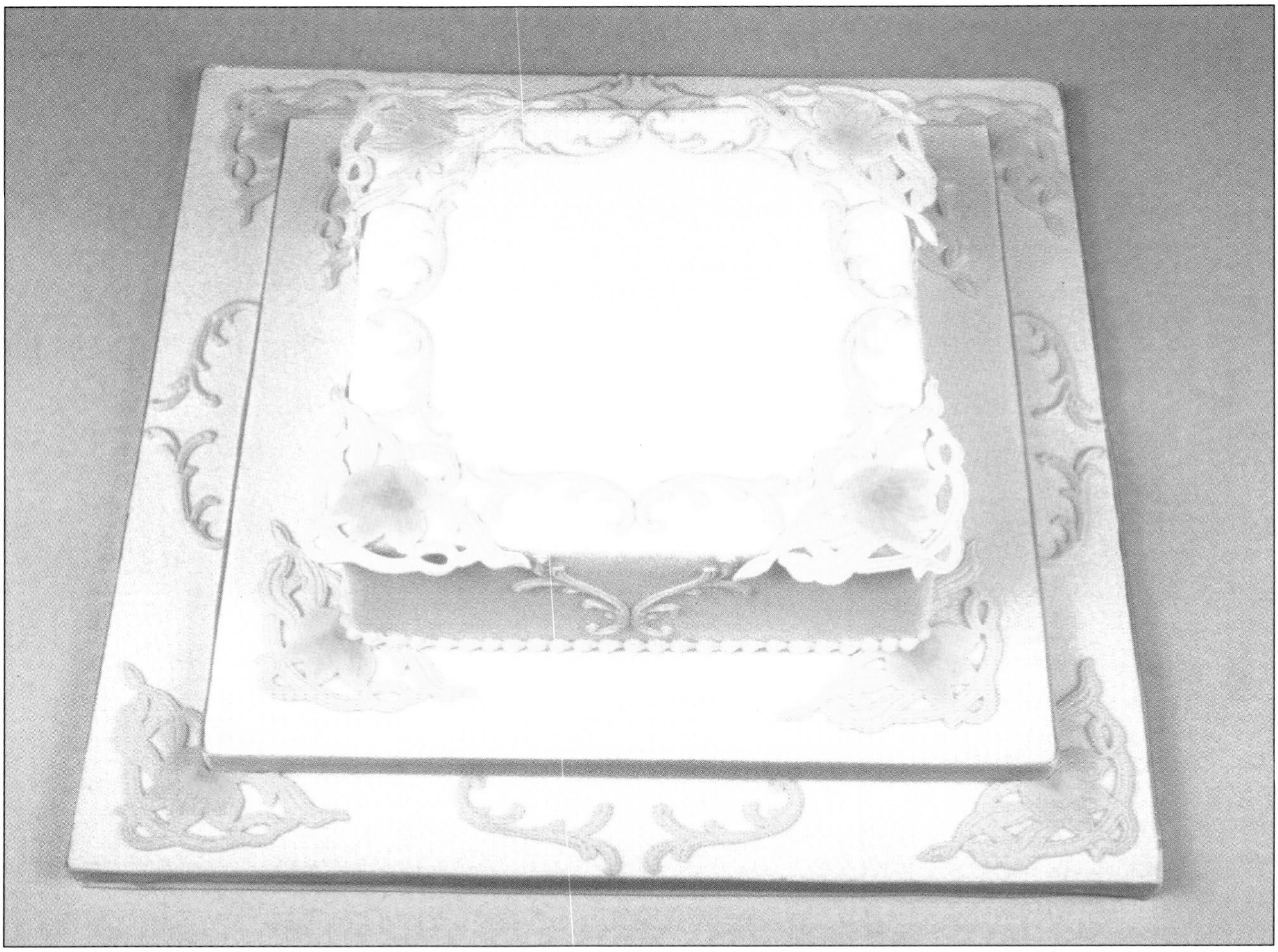

6 The top of the cake showing the Fantasy Cutwork cutter and the double scroll cutter.

7 The side of the cake.

GREYSCALE

BIN TRAVELER FORM

Cut By _Jhonasky_ Qty _25_ Date _11-04-24_

Scanned By _____ Qty _____ Date _____

Scanned Batch IDs

_____ _____ _____

Notes / Exception

_____

_____

_____

_____

_____